ANTI-AGING EXERCISE PLAN

FITNESS SECRETS
OF THE STARS!

Joy Peters, PhD

Order this book online at www.trafford.com
or email orders@trafford.com

Most Trafford titles are also available at major online book retailers.

Print information available on the last page.

ISBN: 978-1-6987-0611-5 (sc)
ISBN: 978-1-6987-0610-8 (e)

Trafford rev. 02/19/2021

Trafford PUBLISHING® www.trafford.com
North America & international
toll-free: 844-688-6899 (USA & Canada)
fax: 812 355 4082

CONTENTS

CHAPTER 1

Exercise is The Real Anti-Aging Pill

Exercise is a repetitive action repeated to work muscles for the purpose of improving the strength, definition and tone of a muscle. An ideal longevity workout plan is comprehensive to work all of the muscle groups within your body and it will include exercises that improve the six essential components: flexibility, mobility, strength, cardio, endurance and recovery. Look no further, this exercise plan has it all, plus it helps tighten, tone and lift your body and face to prevent typical age related sagging so you look more youthful at any age. Most age-related physical appearance problems can be solved with anti-aging exercise practices. The solution is at your fingertips within the following pages of this book!

Have you ever wondered why all those celebrities look years younger than their age? Part of the secret is in how they exercise. Technically, exercise is any deliberate repetitive motion repeated until fatigue of the working muscles is used in the motion. People who exercise feel happier and look more attractive and youthful. People who exercise tend to have longer, healthier lives and according to research exercise is the real anti-aging medicine because it turns on the repair mechanisms of the body all the way down to a cellular level.

Exercise refines the appearance of your body, makes you look lean, fit, attractive and yes, it even makes you sexier. Exercise improves your posture, keeps your cholesterol, and blood pressure in a healthier range, strengthens muscles and improves not only cardiovascular function but also almost every other part of the body including the brain, immune system and energy production systems within the individual cells. Exercise expends energy and generates energy on a metabolic level.

"The #1 Celebrity Anti-Aging Secret Is That Exercise Is The Real Anti-Aging Pill!"

Exercise Is The Real Anti-Aging Pill

Think of exercise as a medicine, before you reach for a pill, take your daily dose of exercise as a preventative therapy prescribed in a specific 30 minute dose for a specific need. Exercise is your Anti-Aging Rx.

Why Exercise?

Exercise is not a waste of time and energy. Regular exercise burns stored body fat and improves your energy and overall physical fitness. It also helps reduce stress, improves digestion and elimination, increases endurance and energy levels, promotes lean body mass. There are many types of exercise to target stubborn areas to gain specific results.

The Importance Of Exercise

As you may already know, exercise is important for a healthy mind and body. Exercise not only improves your physical fitness but it improves your mental fitness, as well. Exercise is a great stress reliever and it's important in healthy lifelong weight management. The Mind Body Exercise plan will help increase your balance, flexibility, strength and endurance. The Anti Aging exercise plan works as a mind-body fitness exercise program with any healthy lifestyle plan that you are following, including keto and is especially effective when combined with a balanced diet and nutritional program.

Anti-Aging Exercise

Exercise has many Anti-Aging benefits. Research studies show that short bursts of high intensity intervals of exercise are proven to help your body produce growth hormone. Growth hormone can help your body regenerate and look years younger with the added benefit of helping to reverse some of the signs of aging. Exercise helps you look and feel more youthful.

The Fountain Of Youth Exercises

Frankly, exercise is the best anti-aging pill. Exercise stimulates growth hormone which has an effect to reverse aging. People who exercise regularly without over stressing tend to look ten years younger than their actual age. But there are specific exercises that the youthful effects seem magical. For example, legend has it that people in the remote reaches of the Himalayan mountains lie as secret mind-body exercises that generations of Tibetan monks have passed down.

These exercises are said to be a fountain of youth. It is a series of simple exercises with age-reversing qualities. The" Tibetan Rites of Rejuvenation" are five one-step secret exercises. The five exercises are simple and greatly resemble yoga postures.

It only takes just minutes a day to perform these exercises and the benefits include increased energy, weight loss, better memory, new hair growth, pain relief, better digestion and feeling younger. However, there are other methods with similar effects. As a certified personal trainer, for over 20 years, I have devised 3 modern exercises that anyone can do in their home, at work or practically anywhere in 15-30 minutes.

These exercises can be modified from beginner to advanced level exercises, starting out for beginners and working your way up over time to more reps and by adding weights. These are simple exercises that anyone can perform in a matter of minutes.

These quick and easy exercises help restore youthful health and vitality by improving physical strength and flexibility additionally helping to improve balance and the mind-body connection to harmonize energy within the body while increasing your core strength and total body muscle tone over time with exercise and a healthy diet and lifestyle system.

What Celebrities Do To Stay Super Star Fit

The celebrity job market is super competitive, that is one reason they have to keep a super fit body. It is their job to look good to play their characters roles in film and television.

My whole career has revolved around keeping close tabs on cutting edge developments in anti-aging and the outcomes of newly released research studies results involving genetics and age research and from the 20+ years that I've worked with celebrity clients I have discovered many things in helping them achieve their health and image goals. I have provided services to many of the top celebrities in the world and I can tell you for certain, they keep a close check on their body composition and their daily lifestyle by following a strict daily regime. They are dedicated to only consuming the right amount of calories and not exceeding their recommended caloric intake to maintain their goal weight. Also, they exercise daily, and alternate their workouts and make exercise a fun part of their lifestyle. They work with personal trainers, life coaches, psychologists, agents and managers to stay on track. They do pilates and yoga and they use the services of nutritionists and some even have a personal chef or an assistant to manage their meals, beauty treatment schedules down to giving them their daily nutritional supplements and medications each day, on time. They see body workers, massage therapists. They go to health retreats, spa-resorts, med-spas and yes, plastic surgeons. However, with these times of high technology and dermal fillers, many celebrities avoid the knife and go with more natural options, too. They have yoga instructors that teach body and face lifting yoga exercises and facialists that do special facial lifting techniques, which I share with you in the face care section of this book so you can do them, too.

Super Fit People Are Super Attractive

Super Star A-List Body

Celebrities keep a body that is extremely fit because being fit makes them so much more attractive and sexier and gives them a leading edge in auditions when they are seeking a part in a film and when they are performing. The better they look the more it helps them advance in their career because it's every celebrity's goal to become an A-lister. A-listers are the cream of the crop so to speak as celebrities are rated.

Celebrity Public Statements On Exercise Habits

- **Charlize Theron**- "It's all about making fitness fun". She has openly said that she does two sessions of power yoga weekly, pilates and spin classes.
- **Jason Momoa**- the Aquaman says, swimming can be boring and that it is like going on a treadmill. So to mix it up he likes to get some of his exercise from outdoor sports instead of only doing a repetitive regime in the gym.

- **Gwen Stefani**- works out at least four times a week, for 60-75 minutes per session, doing high-intensity weight training combined with cardiovascular training but singing, burns a lot of carbs, yes, singing! Everytime we exhale, we release carbs and carbonic acid as we breathe out. Additionally, singing requires muscle control in upper diaphragm and core.
- **Scarlett Johansson**- Exercise practice includes, integrated foundational strength training, plyometrics, yoga, weight lifting, and kettlebells.
- **Justin Timberlake**- "You're not meant to do what is easy. You're meant to challenge yourself". He gets exercise from dance, weightlifting, sports, and singing, regularly.
- **Tom Cruise**- switches up his cardio and strength work with something like fencing or climbing. He does most of his own stunts and displays incredible self-discipline in his fitness and health regimens. He is focused and motivated and is one of the most incredible celebrities, in my opinion, it is his competitive spirit and determination to be a success in all things.
- **Dwayne Johnson**- The Rock works out six days a week. He starts off with 30-50 minutes of cardio before moving on to strength building later in the day. He enjoys high-energy wrestling. Afterall, he is a former WWF champion who won the championship five times!
- **Rocky/Sylvester Stalone-** Sly trains twice a day and focuses on forearms, traps, and shoulders with a combo full body workout of strenuous exercises and squats. He is "Rocky", to play the character, he became a real fighter, he stays in tip-top fighting shape to play his roles.
- **Paris Hilton**- during the 2020 Covid outbreak, released a Tic-Toc exercise post of herself doing bicep curls with her designer handbags and used her staircase stating, "staircases are hotter than gym stairmasters" aside from that she stays active as a DJ and dancing along to all of her 2-4 hour DJ gigs and burns off a lot of calories.

There are celebrities all around the world and the celebrity capitol of the world is Hollywood When you walk down the walk of fame on the streets of Sunset boulevard, you'll see the stars on the street emblazoned with the names of the most famous celebrities and with each step you take you realize each of those celebrities relied on their appearance and physical fitness to stay at the top of the entertainment industry.

At the center of Hollywood is the Grauman's Chinese theater where all super-star status celebrities have entombed their hand and shoe prints in cement along with their autograph signatures. You can rest assured knowing each of those elite mega-stars live a lifestyle that revolves around preserving their aesthetic appearance and beauty. Most celebrities fill their' days with self-care consisting of daily exercise and aesthetic services, although many have alluded to plastic surgery, many of today's celebrities forgo the knife and rely on an extreme fitness regimen, anti-aging treatments and anti-aging hormone replacement therapies to stay in tip-top shape.

Steroids And Growth Hormone Options

Many celebrities and bodybuilders have used growth hormones to reverse the hands of time and steroids to bulk up their muscles, yet, there are alot of harmful side effects in taking synthetic steroids and growth hormones. The good news is, there are legal and natural alternatives to steroids and often peptides such as sermorelin work as effectively as prescription growth hormones without the dangerous side effects of off-label use of injectable growth hormones. Creatine is the only natural steroid that the Food and Drug Administration (FDA) approves for short-term use in healthy adults aged over 18 years to improve athletic performance. The following are a few other options to enhance and aid in building your muscles and that trigger the molecules of youth, naturally.

Natural Steroids

- Creatine
- Pine Pollen
- Bee Pollen
- Ashwagandha
- 5-alpha-hydroxy-laxogenin
- Tribulus terrestris
- D-aspartic acid (DAA)
- Vitamin D
- Magnesium
- DHEA
- A-Z Amino Acids Multi

- Alanine/ Carnosine
- Zinc

Natural steroids help with:

- improving endurance
- improving strength
- increasing exercise efficiency
- increasing tolerance for increased intensity training
- achieving an athletic looking body goal more quickly

Alternatives To Growth Hormones:

There are many different growth hormones. The most commonly known in the fitness arena is Human Growth Hormone (HGH) as it helps to maintain and build muscle. Also, HGH is good for anti-aging as it helps repair healthy tissue in the brain, skin and other organs. This hormone can help to speed up healing after an injury and repair muscle tissue after exercise. HGH helps to build muscle mass, boost metabolism, and burn fat. HGH is also said to benefit the quality and appearance of the skin.

The following are evidence-based ways to increase human growth hormone (HGH) levels naturally:

- Exercise at a high intensity
- Take a Multi-Amino
- Lose body fat
- Fast intermittently
- Try an Arginine supplement
- Reduce your sugar intake
- Don't eat a lot before bedtime
- Take a GABA supplement
- Take beta-alanine
- Take anti-aging brand peptides
- Drink a collagen peptide sports drink with your workouts
- Follow a health balanced diet and lifestyle plan
- Make sure your diet is friendly to anti-aging
- Take Melatonin before bed to optimize your beauty sleep

CHAPTER 2
Results, Habits and Motivation

Shared Success & Visible Results

Your appearance will improve with exercise. As your looks and health improve from using the 3 simple Anti-Aging exercises in chapter 9, you will see success and others will notice your physique and it may inspire others around you to seek to reach their health and fitness goals, too.

Exercise Helps You Look And Feel Your Best

Those who exercise and maintain their physical fitness tend to be healthier, stronger and are more attractive than their sedentary counterparts. Exercise improves your physical appearance, stamina and endurance which parallels a state of good health and well being. Daily exercise can increase your energy levels and may provide a sense of super-star, energy and help you look like a celebrity, too.

There is nothing stopping you from being as physically fit as a celebrity. It is a choice. Set the time of day that you will work out daily at home, now. All it takes is one 30 minute daily home exercise routine a day. Think of how you will feel in 30 days.

What Time Is Your Daily Home Exercise Appointment?

Home Exercise Importance

All of these exercises can be done at home and offer a simple solution for doing exercise in a small space and may be a great asset to your self-improvement goals. These Anti-Aging exercises benefit both your mind and body in one complete exercise program. It is a home anti-aging practice for anyone striving to achieve better physical fitness and will help to improve your overall general health and physical strength, too. Anti-Aging exercises will give you a positive change that enables you to reach your fitness goals by following these principles to see quick results that you will likely want to do, forever. Share as you learn so your friends and family can enjoy the benefits of better health with you. It is important for everyone. We found also that this is a perfect exercise plan for those who were under shelter-in-place order during the pandemic. The program helps anyone, anywhere, stay physically fit. When you share and teach others, this method, you also are contributing to the improvement of the health of yourself, your friends and family.

Consider Exercise As A Reward To Yourself

Each day there are things we must do that are not considered fun, by some people's standards. It's always a good idea to do what you love and love what you do. The rest of the time we go to work, go to school, clean up the house and yard, take out the trash, do laundry, cook and clean but doing a daily exercise routine is a fun 'me-time' activity. Consider exercise as a reward for doing a good job on some chore or work project.

Exercise is fun, it's not a chore. Choose something you enjoy or related to what you enjoy. For example, if you decide you want to take up a new hobby, say for example, it is winter, but, in the spring you know you want to learn to kayak in the waters of the great outdoors, therefore choose rowing as your daily home exercise. A daily rowing machine workout will prepare your body for when you do hit the water in a kayak in the spring. Knowing you are conditioning your body for a great future experience is very motivational and your rowing exercise routine then becomes an inspiration to keep you motivated to do your daily exercise routine and reap the reward in the future.

Do What You Love & Love What You Do

Each of us can make a difference by making an individual conscious decision to improve our own fitness lifestyle and personal health. Just as your individual efforts are important in improving your personal health status, becoming and staying physically active is imperative to good health and will help to improve your future health. Sedentary lifestyle is detrimental to health and it's important to exercise while you shelter-in-place. So with that being said let us explore the logistics of exercise.

American Exercise Habits:

Less than one-third of adults in the United States are currently getting the recommended amount of physical activity to stay healthy, physically fit and trim. The Department of Health and Human Services recommends adults get at least 150 minutes of moderate aerobic activity or 75 minutes of vigorous aerobic activity a week or a combination of moderate and vigorous activity. In other words, the human body needs to be worked on daily.

The Only Thing That Stops People From Becoming Their Best Self Is Themselves...

Making Exercise A Habit

Humans are creatures of habit, anything that you do for 21 days becomes a habit, so choose a set time in your day to do these exercises for 21 consecutive days. It is important to set a schedule and stick to it. It is a program that is also suitable to be included with other workout or exercise routines depending on your fitness goals as your physical strength and endurance increases and you move into more activities that are physical.

Exercise Rule #1– "Never allow yourself to fall into the sedentary lifestyle category, stay-in and stay safe but stay active!"

Get Motivated

Post a picture of a physically fit mentor or yourself when you were at your most physically fit peak. Post these pictures on your refrigerator door, on your bathroom mirror and on your front door so that you see it each day before you start your day and each night before you go to bed. Remind yourself constantly of how you want to look and feel. This is a mental exercise. Physical exercise is important to your weight loss and permanent weight loss. Before beginning any new exercise program, always see your doctor for medical clearance. Seek advice from your physician if you are pregnant or nursing before beginning any exercise program.

Doing The Work = Reaping The Reward

Think It's Hard To Exercise?

Exercise does not have to be strenuous to be beneficial. Studies show that short sessions of exercise are effective and that several short sessions are just as good as one long session of exercise. Most adults should get a minimum of 30 minutes of moderate physical activity and children should get an hour of moderate exercise daily.

How Long Before I See Results

Most people report seeing results quickly and that they look younger than their age when they do these exercises and you should, too. I also guarantee if you don't exercise your body will age quickly and you will look older than your age if you never exercise. You can start to see results within a few days and your body begins to tighten and tone. Dramatic improvement can be seen within 21 days of starting this exercise routine. Make it part of your life and don't ever stop.

Get Motivated

Post a picture of a physically fit mentor or one of yourself when you were at your most physically fit peak. Post these pictures on your refrigerator door, on your bathroom mirror and on your front door so that you see it each day before you start your day and each night before you go to bed. Remind yourself constantly of how you want to look and feel.

This is a mental exercise. Life is movement. Physical exercise is important to your weight loss and permanent weight loss. Before beginning any new exercise program, always see your doctor for medical clearance. Seek advice from your physician if you are pregnant or nursing before beginning any exercise program.

Musculoskeletal System

Your whole internal body is covered by a protective layer of muscle. As a whole your skeletal muscle is considered an organ of the muscular system. Each organ or muscle consists of skeletal muscle tissue, connective tissue, nerve tissue and blood or vascular tissue. Skeletal muscles vary considerably in size, shape, and arrangement of fibers. The muscular system is attached at origin and origination points that distinguish the various muscles and muscle groups.

Exercise Targets & Tones Specific Muscles

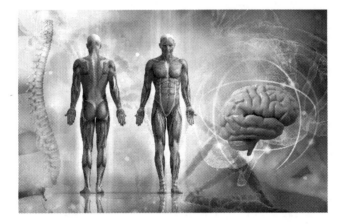

Exercise Is Beneficial For Total Fitness

Exercise is for muscle health, brain health and bone health. Weight bearing exercises and weight lifting helps build muscles and bones. Your spine needs flexibility exercise, too.

First Step Track Your Progress In A Journal

Prepare to track your progress and success. Weigh and measure yourself. Record every time you do this exercise in a personal journal. Track your progress and write it in a journal or you can use the form you will find in the back of this book. Take some before, during and after selfies and post them on social media.

Life Is Movement, Don't Stop Moving Until Your In The Grave

How To Change Habits With Behavior Modification

The biggest health problem in America stems from a sedentary lifestyle. The Mind Body Weight Loss CD by Dr. Joyce Peters, is not only for weight loss, it contains a track on exercise motivation that you may greatly benefit from as it is layered with subliminal messages that quickly helps program your mind with motivation to exercise. It is safe and effective. Behavior modification is an important step in changing your exercise habits. Why? Because it takes 21 days to form a new habit and for a new neural network to connect in the brain to form a new habit from a repetitive action, such as doing 30 minutes of exercise a day. Once you make it through the first 21 days, exercise becomes a habit. You can order this audio quickly on ebay or youtube and start changing your exercise mindset and habits, right now!

Get Out Of The Way, Stop Blocking Your Own Path To Fitness Success

How To Stay Motivated

The number one reason people say they don't exercise is because they don't feel motivated enough. The Mind Body Weight Loss CD by Dr. Joyce Peters, is not just for weight loss, it contains a track on exercise motivation that may help you get motivated to exercise, quickly as it is layered with subliminal messages that quickly helps program your mind with subliminal messages that encourage and motivate you to exercise. It is a safe and effective way to stay motivated to do your daily exercise, just listen to the track each night before bed and wake up feeling refreshed and ready to start your day with exercise.

Mental Preparation Tips:

- Have a Plan and Develop a strategy
- Set a time, make a daily schedule and stick to it.
  - Pick an activity you like
  - Develop a routine.
  - Be Dedicated
  - Be Committed

- Be Disciplined
- Be Passionate
- Be Tenacious

Keep the Big Picture in Mind. Never Give Up & Never Quit. See Yourself Victorious and Physically Fit.

Make A Plan

To be successful you need a strategy regarding implementing your daily fitness plan. Take your physical fitness seriously. Being physically fit will improve your appearance, your quality of your life and health and help in the prevention of disease and illness and even prolong your longevity. Exercise can provide you with a greater quality of life and greater opportunities.

Tips for exercise success:

- Choose an exercise that you enjoy and that you can do on a daily basis without skipping.
- Know and accept that exercise is a mandatory part of staying slender and physically fit.
- Know that being active is the only way to achieve physical fitness and how important it is to get in the habit of being more active.
- Join a gym, exercise or yoga class. If you cannot join a gym, make a commitment to yourself to stick to your personal exercise routine.
- Recruit a reliable, dependable and accountable neighbor or friend as your exercise partner.
- Have a weekly accountability meeting with your exercise partner to monitor your weekly results.
- If your accountability partner is allowing you to slide without opposition, select a new partner.

Other Tips

- Invest in good footwear, gym clothes and workout gear.
- Use a daily planner to stay on course with your workouts
- Find a mentor who is dedicated, determined and dependable to work out with.
- Be self motivated, even when others fall off track with their exercise routine.

Staying Committed To Your Exercise Routine

Sticking to an exercise routine takes practice, stamina, determination and dedication. Exercise can become a habit. If you exercise for 21 days in a row it can become a habit. The good news is that it is one of the healthiest habits you can develop to stay physically fit, agile, youthful and happy. Start slowly, select three or four exercises that suits your needs and that you enjoy and incorporate a time during your day to do your exercises. Set an alarm to remind yourself to do them at this specific time. Choose exercises that you can do no matter where you are. You don't have to be at a fancy gym to exercise. Although I do recommend joining a gym or health club for motivation. It can be very motivating watching others exercise or exercising in groups with others.

CHAPTER 3

Exercise as A Healthcare Prescription

Nothing else you can do will improve your health and well being better than exercise. Exercise strengthens your heart and improves your circulation. Increased blood flow raises oxygen levels in your body. This helps lower your risk of heart diseases, high cholesterol, coronary artery disease, and heart attack.

Better Health & Well Being

Regular exercise can also lower your blood pressure and triglyceride levels. Exercise extends your life and longevity. Exercise gives you better quality of health and a better sense of wellbeing.

Exercise Integrated Into HealthCare

On your next visit to the doctor, you may receive one of the most important prescriptions you'll ever receive, one that only you can fill, by doing daily exercise. Research shows a sedentary lifestyle kills. Being sedentary actually accelerates aging. Doctors all across the world are catching the exercise bug because hundreds of studies show that exercise lowers your risk for serious health problems, including reducing the risk for heart disease, diabetes, stroke, high blood pressure, and certain forms of cancer. Exercise also, eases arthritis and preserves your independence as you age. A sign of ill health is a large abdomen. Exercise is key to slimming down your waistline. As always, it is recommended that you see your doctor before starting any new exercise program, especially, if you have pre-existing physical limitations.

"No pain, No gain!"

Who Can Do This Exercise Plan?

This exercise plan is suitable for all age groups of both genders. How is that possible? The strongest people may add weights to this routine and increase the repetitions as their body gets stronger and weaker or less physically fit individuals may decrease the repetition and take longer breaks in between while gradually working their way up to more advanced levels. This program may help you and many people across the country achieve a healthier state of health and well being with a healthier lifestyle practice, such as exercise, during this time of shelter-in-place and beyond, because you can do these exercises throughout life to strengthen your body and calm your mind.

Medical Clearance For Exercise

In this day of tele-medicine, you can have an online medical visit quickly. Although these types of exercises are simple and typically safe, physical ability varies in each individual so keep this in mind as you start these exercises for the first time. If you have pre-existing conditions a checkup is mandatory. Additionally, if you've never adhered to an exercise plan you will benefit from a fitness trainer for instructions to avoid risk of sports injuries. For the rest of us, it is important to take any new exercise regime slow and be mindful of the motions you make with your body ensuring a proper posture and body mechanics so that you don't injure yourself. Always be cautious not to over exercise the first day and build up repetitions as your strength increases over time. You may be tempted to over exercise the first day because they are so easy to do. If you should experience any discomfort, stop exercises and correct your positioning. The attage, "no pain, no gain" is incorrect.

Exercise Is Never Supposed
To Be Painful

Medical View Of Mind Body Methods

Top colleges, such as Harvard, now offer training in mind-body medicine as a therapeutic exercise and healthy lifestyle practice. Two of the most popular are qigong and thai-chi. Both exercise practices are recognized as valid assets that help to improve physical and mental health. Medical professionals are now successfully incorporating mindfulness practices and wellness exercises into healthcare plans. In the future of medicine, more of these types of eastern wellness practices are expected to be integrated into western medicine as they are proven to offer lasting health improvements.

Exercise Safety

Avoid injury, always stretch, warm up and cool down. Do not pull on your own neck for leverage when doing a sit-up, use your abs, only, do not bend your neck or back or apply pressure to the back of the head during floor exercises. Keeps the neck posture in a good position straight at all times during all of these exercises. Keep your toes straight ahead to reduce knee and plantar stress, except while in squat position and keep your toes up distributing weight to the back of the heels. If you notice any discomfort stop exercising and correct positioning before resuming any exercise. As with any exercise routine see your doctor for medical clearance before starting any new exercise routine. A fitness trainer may help to ensure proper positioning and help to maximize the effects of your exercise routine and help you avoid injury. Sore muscles are often a side effect of any new exercise plan. There are a couple of natural things that help prevent sore muscles:

- Drink plenty of water to flush out lactic acid and reduce soreness from exercise.
- Take a magnesium supplement to help prevent sore muscles
- Stretch before and after exercising.

Mild Muscle Soreness Is
A Normal Side Effect Of Exercise

Normal Muscle Symptoms After Exercise:

- You may not notice any immediate difference
- Muscle fatigue

- Muscle tension
- Muscle twitching
- Muscle soreness

Muscle Symptoms Consult With A Doctor:

- Heart palpitations,
- Elevated heart rate at rest
- Chest tightness
- Chest pain
- Muscle pain
- Muscle spasms or cramps

The Role Of Exercise In Weight Management

Exercise is important in weight loss and in weight management. If you diet without adequate exercise, oftentimes, you will experience a phase of weight loss of ten pounds followed by a phase where you hit-a-wall and it may seem that you cannot lose any more weight. This wall is known as the base metabolic rate set point. This occurs when you have reached your memorized fat storage, which is not necessarily the healthiest level of fat storage. To restart your fat burning and fat- loss increase your calories of healthy protein and good fats a little and increase exercise and activity level, until your break through the wall and weight loss resumes. This tricks the body's fat set point to lower and it is the only solution known to help you break away from the programmed fat set point and establish a new one. Exercise will recalibrate your set point and jumpstart the metabolic rate to continue the fat burning process. When you hit that wall and feel like you are not losing weight, increase your exercise, it will quickly help you to break through the wall and help you to resume losing excess fatty weight.

Improving Anxiety And Stress With Exercise

These exercises are not only for anti-aging they are good for both your mind and body. The goal of these types of mind-body exercises are not only designed to improve your physical fitness, they may also help ease stress and anxiety. Exercise helps your body produce endorphins and others feel good hormones that offset stress hormones and help you feel better in general. As you transform your body into a stronger, leaner physique with these exercises it can help lower stress hormones, stress is known as the silent killer because the stress hormones trigger a cascade of detrimental effect on the organ systems of the body and can lead to age related conditions such as high-blood pressure. The good news is these exercises may lower your risk of adult onset illnesses and these exercises make an effective addition to a healthy lifestyle to transform your out-of-shape body into a healthier body image and with continued use it may help you maintain physical fitness for a lifetime. "Mind-Body exercises" can help you transform your body and ease your stress as you achieve your health and fitness goals.

Better Health & Improved Mood Are Normal Side Effects Of Exercise

Sedentary America

The rate of sedentary lifestyles in America is alarming. Most American adults do not engage in physical activity during leisure time. The lack of physical activity is very high in the United States according to a report by the National Center for Health Statistics. It is estimated that over forty percent of American adults are not physically active in any form of physical exercise program. This report also indicates that women are more sedentary than men and that children are more sedentary than ever before.

Fact #1- A sedentary lifestyle is destructive to your health and can cause you to age more quickly so always stay active and especially during winter season when you're stuck inside a lot or even during times of shelter-in-place orders. You can still stay flexible and physically fit during those times that you have to stay inside and you will become stronger by doing these daily exercises. When weather or outside conditions mandate that you stay indoors.

You Can Do This Exercise Plan Anywhere In Just 30 Minutes A Day. No Excuses!

Minimum Exercise Requirements

According to the American College of Sports Medicine, every adult should exercise a minimum of 30 minutes of moderate intensity exercises on a daily basis to maintain healthy weight, good health, proper posture and muscle tone.

Recognize these important exercise facts:

- Recognize that deciding to exercise is a choice you make on a daily basis.
- Recognize you must set a specific appointment time to exercise daily.

- Recognize that exercise accountability can help keep you motivated and on track with your weight management goals.
- Recognize that any exercise is better than no exercise at all.
- Recognize that exercise in the morning speeds up metabolism for the whole day, all day
- Recognize that exercise is a necessary part of any healthy lifestyle and weight management program.
- Recognize that exercise improves the body physically and psychologically.
- Recognize that exercise makes you look and feel great.
- Recognize that exercise is one of the best ways to stay youthful
- Recognize that exercise gives you the physical endurance and strength to stay active.

C H A P T E R 4

How To Get & Stay Motivated

Get Motivated And Stick-To-It

Ask anyone why they don't exercise. You will hear a similar story that usually sounds something like this. "I am so busy I don't have time to exercise" or "I don't have the energy to exercise". While it is true there are only so many hours in the day, nothing is more important for your health, than exercise.

Exercise Tips To Help You Stay Motivated For Life

The first step is to choose the exercise that is right for you, that you enjoy doing and choose exercises according to your current physical health abilities. Pace yourself so you don't over do it in the beginning. Commit to stick to exercising for the long haul. Use caution not to burnout or give-up. You should exercise a minimum of 30-45 minutes 3 to 5 times per week.

In Life You Will Only Have One Body, & There Is Nothing More Precious Or Valuable Than Your Health And Fitness!

How To Stay Motivated To Exercise

One of the most simple things you can do is schedule in on your daily to-do-list calendar is set your alarm for 30 minutes of exercise at the same time every day.

Keeping A Go & Do Mindset.

- "Keep the "Go & Do" mind-set of your youth.
- Wear protective gear and commit to doing it.
- Youthful people are busy and active.
- Let's work out!
- Work to create the results you desire.
- Become more active.
- Believe in yourself!
- You can do it!
- Impossible is nothing and nothing is impossible.

If inclement weather doesn't permit you to go outside to exercise or if you are under a shelter-in-place order such as with Covid-19, practice social distancing, but keep a go-and-do mindset and lifestyle.

Exercise Improves Emotional and Mental Health

Studies show that exercise is good for the mind. The following is a list of the known positive effects on the mind.

- Exercise has a positive effect on brain function and mood.
- Exercise increases the mental faculties as it increases circulation, blood flow, nutrients and oxygen to the brain while increasing waste removal.
- Exercise increases our ability to multitask, ignore distractions, and respond and react quickly.
- Exercise increases neurotransmitters.
- Exercise gives you an "oxygen high" and neurons function better when they get oxygen.
- Exercise increases alertness and mental energy.

Exercise Pyramid

Think of the varieties of exercises as a pyramid. Some you do daily and other exercises you only need to do 1-3 times per week. The pyramid concept as it serves as a guide to illustrate the hierarchy level of importance of each type of physical activity.

- 1-3 days per week-Weight Lifting/Muscle Building
  (interval training)

- 3-5 days per week-Aerobic, Cardio, Anti-Aging short-burst/high intensity
- 5-7 days per week-Mind-Body Exercises
  (Floor Exercise Routine/Yoga/Pilates)

- 7 days per week-Daily Stretching, Deep Breathing, Walking.

Exercise Pyramid

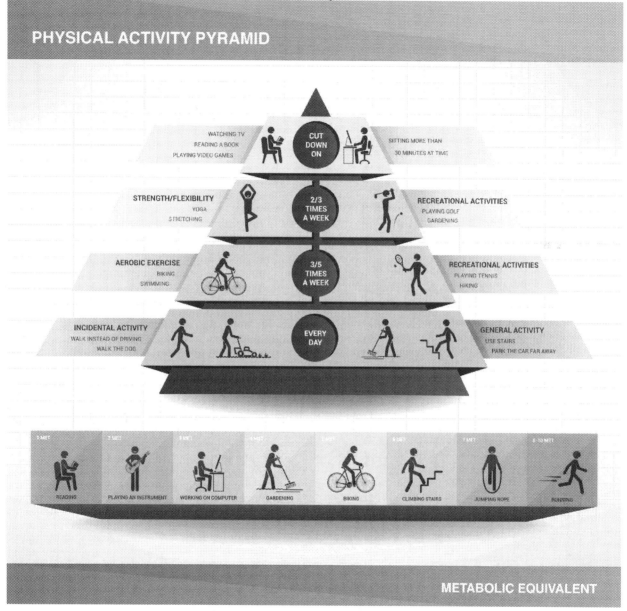

PHYSICAL ACTIVITY PYRAMID

WATCHING TV
READING A BOOK
PLAYING VIDEO GAMES

CUT DOWN ON

SITTING MORE THAN
30 MINUTES AT TIME

STRENGTH/FLEXIBILITY
YOGA
STRETCHING

2/3 TIMES A WEEK

RECREATIONAL ACTIVITIES
PLAYING GOLF
GARDENING

AEROBIC EXERCISE
BIKING
SWIMMING

3/5 TIMES A WEEK

RECREATIONAL ACTIVITIES
PLAYING TENNIS
HIKING

INCIDENTAL ACTIVITY
WALK INSTEAD OF DRIVING
WALK THE DOG

EVERY DAY

GENERAL ACTIVITY
USE STAIRS
PARK THE CAR FAR AWAY

1 MET — READING
2 MET — PLAYING AN INSTRUMENT
3 MET — WORKING ON COMPUTER
4 MET — GARDENING
5 MET — BIKING
6 MET — CLIMBING STAIRS
7 MET — JUMPING ROPE
8-10 MET — RUNNING

METABOLIC EQUIVALENT

Health benefits of exercise are:

- ♥ Loss of excess body fat & weight
- ♥ Helps to burn stored fat into beautiful radiant energy
- ♥ Increased and improved digestion
- ♥ Decreases harmful stress
- ♥ Increase in energy, decreases fatigue
- ♥ Improvement of moods and sense of well-being
- ♥ Increased total blood volume and nutrient assimilation
- ♥ The aerobic capacity increases
- ♥ The muscles including the heart are strengthened
- ♥ Decreases risk of high cholesterol and increased HDL
- ♥ Positive body composition and muscle tone changes
- ♥ Stimulates the excretion of toxins and metabolic waste
- ♥ Improvement of bone density
- ♥ Improves self image, self confidence
- ♥ Increased sense of peace in mind, body & spirit
- ♥ Increased productivity and endurance
- ♥ Increased oxygen to cells, organs, brain and body.
- ♥ Improvement of physiological & psychological fitness
- ♥ Increased libido
- ♥ Decrease in depression
- ♥ Increase chance of longevity

THE CHOICE IS YOURS...

Consequences of a lack of exercise may lead to:

- ∅ Accumulation of fat and excess weight
- ∅ Increase in cellulite in women
- ∅ Increase in apple and pear shaped physique
- ∅ Decrease in hour-glass and trapezoid physique
- ∅ Increased risk of muscle atrophy & disease
- ∅ Increase in infertility, Decreased Libido
- ∅ Decrease in self-esteem
- ∅ Increase in depression
- ∅ Increase in fatigue, decrease in energy
- ∅ Increase risk of cancer, diabetes and heart attack

- ∅ Increase risk of injury
- ∅ Increase in stress
- ∅ Increase in shortness of breath
- ∅ Increase risk of early death

CHAPTER 5

Breathing & Warm Up Exercises

The most simple and beneficial exercises of all are a variety of rhythmic breathing exercises. When we exercise we breathe more deeply, when we do cardio exercises our breathing speeds up and with each exhale we release toxic carbonic acid that helps balance our chemistry. Breathing exercises increase our oxygen levels, greatly. Also, breathing releases carb elimination and may also aid in weight loss and weight management. Plants make oxygen, so be sure to get a daily dose of fresh air and sunshine.

Breathing Exercises

Breathing is an important aspect of all exercise as it helps with oxygen flow to the muscles and detoxification. You can breathe in all the energy of the oxygen and exhale carbonic acid and waste, which is one of the most important ways the body maintains balance in its chemistry to keep homeostasis in balance. Deep breathing, meditation, focus exercises will help in so many ways to enhance the mind-body connection that is so important for good mental and physical health.

Rhythmic Breathing Exercise

A calming breathing exercise brings awareness to the breathing process as it draws your focus toward achieving a calm state of mind. It allows you to remain as relaxed as possible, quieting stress to release tension from the body that would otherwise inhibit performance. Whenever you feel a twinge of tension or discomfort, you can mentally "push" it out of your body as you exhale and relax.

Deep Lung Breathing

If you notice your breathing is short and hurried, slow it down by taking long, slow breaths. Inhale slowly, filling your lungs completely up, then exhale slowly, completely emptying your lungs. Count slowly to five as you inhale, and then count slowly to five as you exhale. As you exhale slowly, pay attention to how your body naturally relaxes. You can purchase my breathing exercise CD on ebay, "The Anti-Aging Mind Body Breathing Exercise Meditation & Weight Loss" CD. It is not just for weight loss. It has 3 powerful guided breathing exercises and loads of information about weight loss and healthy lifestyle management.

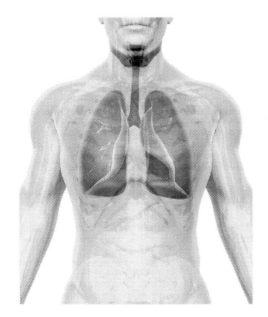

Stress Relieving Deep Breathing

One of the best benefits of yoga breathing exercises is stress relief. Bringing hands to Namaste' position while you raise the upper body up toward the sky bringing yourself up into a sitting position with knees bent, legs open and feet touching sole to sole and hands in prayer position at chest level breathe' in deeply, and exhale slowly, pushing hands above the head in upper Namaste' stretch the spine and dropping your head back as you look up at the sky, breathe in and exhale slowly and repeat. Then bring arms down to rest at the side and calm the mind. Repeat 3 times.

Pranayama Breathing- is a yoga method that revolves around various breathing exercises. Pranayama is a foundational aspect of yoga. Life is breath. Pranayama helps to relieve stress, energize or calm the mind and body. Research shows that a regular pranayama practice can help to relieve symptoms of anxiety, stress and depression.

Some Varieties Of Pranayama Are:

- Alternate nostril breathing (for a more calm sense of well-being)
- Breath of fire (oxygenates the cells, brain and blood)
- Cannon breath (balance the emotions and stimulates focus)
- Sitali breath (calming, cooling and relaxing)
- Vatskar breath (mindfulness, enhancing a "in-the-moment" state of mind, invoking awareness to your presence in the now)

Nostril Breathing Exercise

The left side of the brain activates the right side of the brain where reason and logic is stored. The right brain is rational where the left brain is more emotional and imaginative. In ayurvedic medicine, prayama activates the opposite side of the brain, this type of breathing is particularly effective for compulsive behaviors. If you feel the urge to binge drink get help but also do this exercise:

- Sit in easy pose with a straight spine.
- Block the right nostril with the thumb of the right hand.
- Deeply inhale through your left nostril and fill your lungs.
- Hold a full breath into your longest capacity.
- Then completely exhale through the left nostril
- Hold the breath out for the same amount of time as you held it in.
- Continue to take long deep breaths through the left nostril only and without pressure on your diaphragm for 15-30 minutes.
- Practice daily for 21 days or more as it takes at least 21 days to change a habit and form new neural pathways in the brain helping to break the old habit and replace it with a healthier new habit of breath-work and therefore, this breathing technique can help prevent urges to drink

Remember to do these exercises for 15-30 minutes daily. Make these exercises a part of your daily lifestyle.

Fire Breathing

Fire Breathing or the Breath of Fire is great for increasing your metabolism. This continuous rapid diaphragmatic breathing technique rejuvenates and energizes you. It can be through the nose or mouth. Breathing should be controlled to ensure even balance of each inhalation matching each exhalation. You may become dizzy from an "oxygen high" but with practice overtime, you will master this breathing technique. This is a detoxifying exercise that helps balance body chemistry by excreting carbonic acids with each exhale. This helps to restore balance and homeostasis in the body chemistry enhancing proper nutrient absorption.

- Begin by standing or sitting in Yoga pose.
- Fill your lungs with four deep breaths and as you exhale release all tension from your mind and body. Then quicken the pace of your inhale and exhale cycles as quickly and evenly as possible.
- The rhythmic breathing cycles ebb and flow freely like the tide coming in and going out and your breathing should resemble a see-saw in rhythm, pumping the oxygen in and out of the lungs at an equal pace.

- Keep in mind a soft and tranquil pace while breathing to help in achieving this balance until you reach a state of euphoria. Build up your time and gradually increase to longer periods of fire breathing over time.
- Yoga is a form of endurance training and strength training as well, because most poses allow you to hold the muscle in one pose which increases muscle tone.

Breathing Exercises

Breathing is an important aspect of exercise. Your body must burn energy during physical exertion. Physical exertion increases your heart and respiratory rate. Your body expels energy as carbon dioxide, through your lungs, when you breathe out and your body disposes of fat deposits through a series of complicated metabolic pathways. The byproducts of fat metabolism leaves your body. As water, through your skin when you sweat during exercise and your kidneys when you urinate, usually after exercise.

Sitting Deep Breathing Pose

Instructions:

Sit In Yoga Pose
Knees bent with an open pelvis.
Keep back posture straight
Press soles of feet & palms of hands together.
Inhale Lifting your Diaphragm
Inhale Fill Your Lungs Slowly for 5 seconds
Exhale Breathe Out Slowly for 5 seconds
Repeat. 3 Times

Alternate: you may lay down for deep breathing.

C H A P T E R 6
Stretching for Anti-Aging

Stretching keeps your muscles flexible, strong, and healthy, and we need to maintain youthful flexibility to keep a healthy range of motion in the joints throughout life.

Importance Of Stretching

Without stretching on a daily basis, we begin to lose mobility because the muscles shorten and become tight. Then, when you call on the muscles for activity, they are weak and unable to extend all the way. Therefore, stretching is an anti-aging exercise that needs to be part of your daily lifestyle and fitness routine.

Deep Breathing Torso Stretch

Raise arms overhead open arms and palms

- Lean back slightly to feel your torso muscles stretch
- Inhale- take a long deep breath in.
- Hold for 3 seconds
- Exhale- slowly and Repeat
- Relax.
- Enjoy the feeling.

Repeat 3 Times.

Hamstring, Torso & Lower Back Tension Release

- Lunge on your right leg and feel the stretch in your hamstring, switch sides and repeat.
- Raise your arms overhead, palms together Rotate your pelvis in a circular motion clockwise while adjusting your knees and loosening your joints in the lower back and extremities.
- Repeat the same motion in reverse counter-clockwise.
- Repeat 3-10 times as needed to relax the lower body.

Mind Body Pre Exercise Warm-Up Stretch Routine

Start by standing feet shoulder width apart arms to the side and breathe in as you extend your arms into the air and exhale lowering your arms back down to your sides and release and relax. Focus on any area in your body that you may be experiencing muscle tension. Breath in and with your palm apply gentle pressure and shake your muscle tension vigorously until you feel the stress release from your mind and body.

Warm Up Stretches

- Stretching is the first step before doing any exercise to prepare the body and the muscles and warm them up. Stretching is one of the most important steps that helps prevent injuries.
- Breathing while you stretch increases oxygen saturation to your muscles. Stretching to warm up the muscle groups increases blood flow to your muscles. Proper form, posture and positioning as it is just as important to avoid strain or injury.

Side Bend Stretch

Extend your arm over your head.
Bend sideways to the left side at the waist, feel the stretch in your torso.

- Hold 3 seconds
- Switch sides
- Repeat.
- Relax between sets.

Enjoy the feeling.
Repeat 3 Times.

Side Bend Stretch

Bring one arm at a time above your head and bend at the waist reaching the opposite direction into the sky as you stretch and elongate your body as if you were growing toward the sky, tip the toe on the same side to deepen the side posture stretch. Switch sides and repeat the same procedure. Repeat 3 times.

Pace yourself at a slow, steady and mindful pace to ensure proper muscle function and ideally, perform all within 30 minutes.

Mountain Pose Instructions:

- Stand straight
- Open arms down to your side
- Open palms of hands
- Feet together both ankles touching
- Lean back press your shoulder blades together
- Breathe.
- Inhale in deeply.
- Exhale slowly.
- Feel the stretch.
- Relax.
- Enjoy the feeling.

Repeat 3 Times.

Loosen Up Warm Up & Cool-Down Routine

It is important to warm up before exercise and cool down after exercise. In pre-exercise a warm up gets the blood flowing to warm up your muscles, post-exercise it helps get the circulation flowing to remove lactic acid and prevent soreness. Focus your attention on any remaining muscle tension, focus on becoming relaxed and "loosened-up". Shake your lower body and legs and jiggle them vigorously to loosen up all the muscles in your lower body next jiggle your arms and upper body vigorously to loosen up all the muscles in your upper body. Jiggle the whole body together and get the circulation going and the energy flowing.

Upper Body Stretch

- Clasp your hands together and place them behind your neck.
- Gently bring your elbows together as you drop your head down.
- Feel the gentle stretch in your upper back.
- Open your elbows and arch your upper back forward, as you fully open your chest up arching your middle back open and tilt your head upwards toward the sky.
- Breathe deeply, breathe in all the energies of the universe visualize that you are inhaling the breath of life deep into your lungs.

- Relax and keep a calm expression on your face.
- Feel the gentle stretch in your upper back and diaphragm.
- Squeeze the shoulder blades toward each other.
- Hold your position for three seconds.
- Exhale and
- Release
- Repeat 10 times.

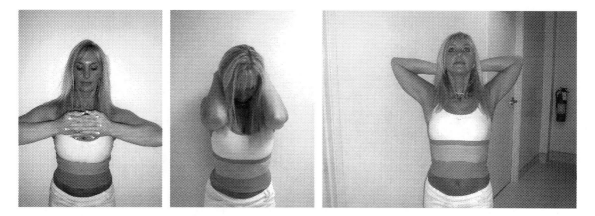

Additional Upper Body Stretch Move:

- Clasp your hands together and place them behind your neck.
- Gently pump your arms like wings in a pumping motion, from front to back 3 times.
- Bring your elbows together as you drop your head down.
- Feel the gentle stretch in your upper back.
- Open your elbows and arch your upper back forward, as you fully open your chest up arching your middle back open your chest up and release tightness and tension in your chest and upper back.
- Tilt your head upwards toward the sky, breathe in filling your lungs and as you inhale the breath of life deep into your lungs, feel the gentle stretch in your upper back and diaphragm.
- Squeeze the shoulder blades toward each other, hold 3 seconds, exhale slowly.
- Mindfully, release all tension and stress and
- Repeat 3 times.

Body Twist & Stretch

With feet still apart and facing forward, twisting from your waist line twist your upper body to the right and hold for 3 seconds and then switch sides and twist your upper body to the left and hold for 3 seconds. Repeat 3 times.

Lower Body Twist Stretch

Bring your feet together and stretch your shoulders and upper back by doing shoulder shrugs and rotations. Rotate the shoulders in a forward motion and a reverse rotation motion three times. Repeat 3 times. Twist your upper body.

The number one exercise fact is:

"Physical activity is needed to stay slim, physically fit and healthy".

CHAPTER 7

Metabolism During Exercise

While exercising keep your metabolism in mind. There are metabolic processes at play in how your body works to produce fuel for energy during exercise. During endurance activity, one major metabolic process is by way of nitrogen being removed from the branched chain amino acids and converted into alanine. Alanine is transported through the bloodstream, from the muscle to the liver where it is converted to glucose.

The liver then returns glucose back into the muscle as fuel in an effort to supply the energy to increase muscle power and performance. The amino acids and neurotransmitters glutamine and Arginine are two amino-acids considered essential during metabolic stress. One of the functions of Glutamine, is to serve as the primary carrier of nitrogen to skeletal muscle and other tissues during exercise. It boosts protein synthesis and helps buffer lactic acid buildup that occurs during exercising. It also reduces central nervous system fatigue.

Several studies have shown that the arginine plays a key role in stimulating the release of anabolic hormones that promote muscle formation. It is also a precursor to nitric oxide, which promotes healthy blood vessels. These amino acids are important in the building, the growth and recovery of the muscle. You can get these amino's in balanced form from consuming protein. Many foods contain these nutrients including soy or whey protein has the more dynamic health benefits and are a preferred source of protein.

Even Short Burst Of Vigorous Exercise Boost Your Metabolism

Metabolic Rate

Your average basal energy expenditure (BEE), also known as basal metabolic rate (BMR), for American women is about 1,400 calories while for a man it is approximately 1,800 and usually, your basal metabolic rate drops roughly one to two percent per decade as you age.

Increase Metabolic Rate With Portion Control

Portion size and portion control are the two most important factors. Too much of a good thing can disrupt your metabolic rate and repeated over-eating will make you fat. Moderation is key for everything in life and especially food. Always eat a normal size portion and remember your stomach is only about the size of your fist the more you stretch it the harder it is to control your appetite and feel full eating a normal sized portion. Exceeding your body's daily caloric requirement disrupts your metabolism. Overeating is never good.

1. Don't Exceed Your Calorie Requirement.
2. Drink More Water.
3. Increase Your Protein Intake.
4. Cut Your Carb Consumption.
5. Start Lifting Weights.
6. Eat More Fiber
7. Set a Sleep Schedule
8. Work out daily
9. Cut out sugar

Body Mass and Weight Index Chart

Body mass index, or BMI, is a new term to most people. However, it is the measurement of choice for many physicians and researchers studying obesity.

- BMI uses a mathematical formula that takes into account both a person's height and Weight.
- BMI equals a person's weight in kilograms divided by height in meters squared. (BMI=kg/m2).
- A BMI of 22-27 is normal for people age 45-54
- A BMI of 23-28 is normal for people age 55-65
- A BMI of up to 29 is normal for people over 65.

According to the BMI scale:

- Healthy weight- BMI from 18.5 up to 25
- Overweight–BMI from 25 up to 30

People with a BMI over 30 are considered obese.

- 30+ BMI = Obese.

Healthy Cosmetic BMI Range

Height	Weight	BMI Range
4'10	91–117	18–20 BMI
5'	102–117	19–22 BMI
5'5	119–137	20–23 BMI
6'	148–170	18–24 BMI
6'4	156–204	21–25 BMI

Metabolism And Fat Burning Target Heart Rate

In order to burn stored fat we have to reach a target heart rate of 120 beats per minute and not exceed 150 beats per minute in order for our exercise to burn stored fat. If we exceed this rate, the fat burning process shuts down. Avoid pushing yourself too hard during the work out because exceeding the "fat burning heart rate" will sabotage the fat burning action of the body by exceeding the fat burning zone.

Calories Burned Based on 30 Minutes of Activity

Based on a 30 minute time frame:
Weight Training-burns off between 160-200 calories depending on the exercise.
Walking- at 4 miles per hour burns 240 calories.
Brisk Walking- at 5 miles per hour burns 290 calories.
Jogging- at 6 miles per hour burns 316 calories.
Running- at 7 miles per hour burns 400 calories.
Cycling- at 10 miles per hour burns 200 calories.
Step Aerobics- burns approximately 300 calories.
Fast Swimming- burns off 300 calories
Kick-Boxing-400 calories.
Fast Dancing-350 calories

Moderate Ballet Dancing–290 calories

Slow Dancing– 175 calories

Sexual Activity– 100-400 calories (varies greatly depending on several factors and the individual)

It is very important in weight loss–to exercise at least 30 minutes to an hour daily. Swimming is very good to exercise for weight loss and is a form of resistance exercise. Walking, Jogging or Running all are an excellent form of exercise for weight loss and is one of the most slimming of all exercises.

30-Minute Morning Lite-Aerobic Exercises

Aerobic exercise is like a magic anti-aging pill that slims your body quickly and beautifully. When doing the "Fast Walk-Jog" keep your heart rate between 120 and 150 to keep your body in the fat burning mode. Be careful not to over exert yourself or go into your maximum full aerobic state because it will stop your fat burning process. If you feel weak, faint or dizzy cease exercise immediately and resume at a slower pace after you feel better. Drink plenty of water during exercise.

Calculate Your Aerobic Fat Burning Heart Rate:

To calculate your specific fat burning light-aerobic heart rates, simply subtract your age from 170, this will give you your peak fat burning light-aerobic heart rate, to determine your fat burning light-aerobic heart rate subtract your age from 160 to calculate your maximum light-aerobic fat burning heart rate subtract your age from 170. To calculate your full capacity cardiovascular maximum aerobic heart rate subtract your age by 220. The maximum cardiovascular heart rate is not necessary for weight loss purposes and in fact can block fat metabolism if your heart rate exceeds your maximum-light aerobic fat burning heart rate, which is lower than your maximum full exertion cardiovascular aerobic heart rate. The least technical and most simple thing to remember is to keep your heart rate between 120 and 150 beats per minute to burn stored fat.

Aerobic Heart Rate Range Values
Minimum & Maximum Light-Aerobic
Fat Burning Heart Rate Ratios Aerobic Max

Heart Rate:	160	170	180	220
Age:	- 35	–35	–35	–35
	125	135	145	195

(ratios based on a thirty-five year old adult)

Mind Body Light Aerobic Exercises:

- **Fast Walk-Jog (alternatively: you may jog in place)**

Begin by walking slow and steady for two minutes; gradually walk as fast as you can without running. At the eight minute mark, add a jog step into your walking pace, never allow the heart to go over 150, stay in fat burning mode, keep doing this up until the twelve minute mark. At the twelve minute mark, slow your pace back down to 120 beats per minute for two minutes, slow down to a fast walk for two minutes and then cool down by walking the last two minutes of exercise. This can be done cross-country or on the treadmill at varying grades of incline.

- **Skipping & Jump-Rope**

Usually known as childhood play activities, these two exercises are fun exercises for children that make exercising more like play-time than adult type exercise and they are easy to do in a small space and at home and adults can do them, too. These exercises offer an added benefit of improved balance and coordination skills.

- **Cardio-Jumping Jacks**

Begin by doing light and easy jumping jacks, jump up bringing your hands over your head while spreading your feet apart in the jump. Next, jump back with your feet together bringing your arms back down to your side. Do this for four minutes then as you continue on the four-minute mark add the following movement on the down jumping jack. On the down, bend your knees going into a squat and pulling your arms down to the front of your body, bending your arms at the elbow while you clench your fist and pull them down to your sides as you squeeze and tighten the muscles in your arms, chest, shoulders and upper body. Do this until the four minute mark and resume doing light jumping jacks for the cool down. Breathe in, Stretch, breathe out, Flex your muscles, breathe deeply and relax your body, and shake-out tightness in your muscles to relax your body after your workout.

CHAPTER 8
Yoga, Balance & Flexibility Exercises

Yoga is an exercise practice that has been used for thousands of years by indian peoples. Yoga can help us keep our flexibility and manage stress throughout a lifetime. Yoga is a series of mind-body exercises that are a very beneficial part of any healthy lifestyle program. People, young and old can benefit from the practice of yoga. Please seek proper positioning from a certified yoga instructor to avoid injury. Not intended for people with neck problems, spinal and muscle weakness, pregnancy or injury. Not recommended for pregnant or menstruating women.

Integrative Yoga

The Mind-Body Exercise program targets "problem areas" with minimum stress to the joints and body with yoga-like movements. It includes pre and post exercise stretches as it utilizes both yoga and traditional exercise techniques. The Mind-Body Miracle Exercises are designed to work each area in 3 sets of 10 repetitions while targeting problem areas. It is important to start out using very low weight. 1-2 pounds per side and gradually work your way up to using more weight and muscle strength and endurance is achieved. Do not use too much weight as these exercises are more about the isometric contraction to slenderize, tighten and tone the body and are not designed to build muscle bulk but if you want to bulk up, add weights and always work within your own range of limits and abilities so that you do not strain your muscles. If you have any medical concerns, talk with your doctor before practicing integrative yoga.

Daily Yoga Meditation Preparation and Stretches

While sitting in yoga pose, in an open-legged sitting position, bring soles of feet together, rest your wrist on your legs, arms open, shoulders straight, maintain good posture and relax your body and mind. Focus your mind and attention on your breathing focus and concentration of your intent. Focus on what you intend to achieve in each yoga session. Internalize an awareness of good posture, health and healing in your daily life. Find your center, focus your mind in your body and breathe this moment in deeply as you concentrate on the present moment and push away thoughts of the past and future. During your complete yoga session remain in this meditative healing state of mind and focus on your breathing throughout your whole yoga session. Upon ending your meditations it is always a good opportunity to say a prayer, too.

- Sitting on the floor, in the yoga pose, place your right hand on your left knee as you twist your torso and gently stretch your mid-lower back. Hold three seconds, rotate and switch sides and repeat.

Qi Gong And Tai Chi

Qi Gong and Tai Chi are mind-body "energy-flowing" exercises that were developed in China in the 12th century and are still practiced by many to this day. All of these

Mind–Body exercises have great health benefits and they have become popular worldwide because of their ability to alleviate stress, improve balance, increase flexibility and improve overall health and provide a greater sense of better health and well being. Qi Gong can be very relaxing and soothing as it involves flowing body motions performed slowly and smoothly with controlled mindful breathing. The act of energy flowing exercises with internal focus helps to bring about increased mental clarity and a more relaxed state of mind. Qi Gong exercises are a foundation in Tai Chi training which is a form of martial arts. Qi gong exercises involve rhythmic breathing along with specific slow movements which enhance a person's awareness and help a person learn to control and direct their own energy. Qi Gong helps open up the energy meridians, these are the same energetic pathways that are stimulated by acupuncture treatments. Qi Gong is a low impact form of exercise that can be suitable for all people, young or old and at any fitness level.

According to medical research studies some of the benefits of mind-body exercises such as yoga, tai chi and Qi Gong may include:

- Decreased stress,
- Decreased anxiety and
- Decreased depression
- Improved mood
- Improved flexibility
- Improved aerobic capacity
- Increased energy and
- Increased stamina
- Improved balance and
- Improved agility
- Improved sleep
- Enhanced immunity
- Stable blood pressure
- Improved joint pain
- Improved symptoms of congestive heart failure
- Improve overall well-being
- Reduce risk of falls in older adults.

Flexibility Warm Up & Cool Down

It is important to warm up before each exercise session and cool down after each exercise session.

Yoga Poses As Shown Left To Right:

1. **Mountain Pose**- Sanskrit: Tadasana

- standing with straight spine and shoulder back with shoulder blades pressed inward toward each other lift heels off floor hold 3 seconds, repeat.

2. **Chair Pose**- Sanskrit: Utkatasana

- standing feet together palms together arms extended overhead, bend the knees to squat.

3. **Toe Touch**-

- feet shoulder width apart bend over to touch your toes without arching upper back.

4. **Knee Touch**-

- bend at the waist with your hands on your knees keeping your back straight.

5. **Plank Pose**-

- lay flat on your stomach arms to the side, lift your head.

6. **Cobra Pose**-

- lay on your stomach, push up from the waist, straighten arms, tilt your head up looking at the sky.

7. **Downward Dog–**

- do a toe-touch walk hands out in front of you and shift weight up onto your tip-toes.

8. **Warrior Pose** -

- lunge with arms raised up and palms together.

Repeat 3 times in 30 minutes.

Mind Body Yoga Program

Yoga is an exercise that originated as an integral part of Mind Body Medicine as well as Ayurvedic and Yogic living practices. Yoga tightens and tones the skin and therefore, is an excellent practice during and after weight loss. Yoga soothes the Mind, Body and Spirit. Yoga allows you to focus on what you intend to achieve in a meditative way during each session. Yoga internalizes an awareness of good posture, health and healing in your daily life. Yoga helps bring balance between the mind and body. Yoga helps you to find your center, focus your mind in your body and breathe each moment in deeply and teaches you present mind consciousness. During yoga you concentrate on the present moment and push away thoughts of the past and future. During your complete yoga session you will remain in a meditative healing state of mind and focus on your breathing throughout your whole yoga session. Yoga is a healing practice with many great health benefits.

There are many types of Yoga; most of them are excellent for weight loss and weight management. Some particular poses work very well in slimming problem areas. Yoga is effective against stubborn cellulite. Yoga is an excellent alternative form of healing that is very suited to the needs of thyroid patients. For beginners, yoga's gentle stretching and emphasis on breathing can be done by almost anyone, and reaps immediate rewards in terms of energy, reduction of stress levels, flexibility and reduction of muscle and joint stiffness, and much more in terms of peace of mind and general harmony.

Practicing yoga is an excellent way to tone muscles, eliminate aches and pains, dramatically reduce stress, increase oxygen and help breathing. While I have also tried to do aerobic exercise, I have found that I look forward to yoga unlike aerobics! And very quickly have very rapid results from practicing even a few times a week. For me, and for many others, yoga is much more than exercise as it brings the mind, body, and spirit into balance. I would recommend finding a good yoga class if you can, but you can also start with a home Yoga Video.

Yoga as an exercise increases flexibility. Flexibility refers to the range of motion or joint mobility. Yoga is excellent to help stretch and lengthen the muscle. It is important for any training program to include stretching because it warms up the muscles to help prevent injury. Yoga is useful in increasing flexibility to the spine and can help you maintain youthful mobility. As we age it is common for our body to develop a decrease in flexibility or hypo mobility due to a decrease in activity. If we make it a habit to practice yoga on a regular basis, we can maintain the flexibility of our youth.

Yoga helps to prevent shortening of muscle tendons that are a result from inactivity, muscular asymmetry, age and disease. The regular practice of yoga can be considered as prevention from sprain/strain and hyperextension type injury because Yoga increases flexibility in healthy muscle and ligament tonus and improves joint flexibility. Yoga incorporates static & ballistic stretching as well as proprioceptive neuromuscular facilitation (PNF).

Yoga Toe Touch Stretch

This yoga pose exercise is easy, basically, bend over and touch your toes. Once you master this pose you can make it more interesting as you may also use a block under heels or toes for a greater stretch and enhanced balance.

Flexibility Exercises- as shown in following images:

- Yoga Sitting
- Toe Touch
- Child's Pose
- Cobra Pose
- Kneel Pose
- Lunge Pose
- Side Lunge
- Warrior Pose
- Toe Touch
- Knee Back Twist
- Crawl Pose Extremity Lift
- Squat Thigh Stretch

Downward Dog

One of the most common standing yoga poses is the downward dog. It's a toe-touch with your feet shoulder-width apart. Basically, it's easy, you bend over and touch the floor with your fingertips and your feet are spread wide apart. Once you go into downward dog yoga pose, you can get creative and rock up on tips of fingers and toes or twist at the waist for a better stretch. Hold the pose for 5 to 10 seconds and repeat. This reverses gravity and helps to drain the organ systems of accumulated toxins. Next, Lower heels to the floor bring hands together, clasping fingers together to mimic scooping motion as though you were scooping up the earth's energy up by cupping both hands as you roll each vertebra of your spine slowly up from the root chakra. (optional raise leg and point toe up as high as you can into the air toward the sky)

Yoga Toe Touch & Twist

Keeping the spine straight while you fold your upper body forward at the waist, reaching out in front of you as you lower your upper body slowly down toward the earth. Spread your legs moving feet slightly further than shoulder width apart, as you bring your arms over your head and touch the ground in front of you.

Toe Touch Twist:

Stand up with feet shoulder width apart.

- Bend slowly at the waist forward.
- Flatten the lower back.
- Spread the hips
- Open the legs wide.
- Lower the torso
- Touch the opposite hand to your toes.
- Twist the torso to the right.
- Feel the stretch.
- Hold for 1–3 seconds.
- Switch sides.
- Repeat.

Enjoy the feeling.
Repeat 3 Times.
Relax.

Three Minute Shoulder Sarvangasana Yoga Pose

Known as sarvangasana and pronounced simply, "Asana". The benefits of this pose are numerous. It helps with metabolism, digestion and weight loss. It is also very good for your posture and as a preventative health practice to guard against infections, hypertension, thyroid, irritability, sleeplessness, and shortness of breath, constipation and urinary disorders. It increases strength and balance.

- Arch your body upwards onto your shoulders and extend your legs, touching your toes to the floor over your head, hold for three seconds, flex toes inward stretching the back and hamstrings and then release, relax and repeat 3 times.

Sarvanga Yoga Pose

Sarvanga is an excellent pose to aid in weight loss but also is good for many purposes. In Ayurveda, "Sarva" means the whole, "Anga" means body. Hence, the "Sarvanga" is the whole body. The name means that the whole body benefits from these poses. However, some poses are not recommended for everyone. See your doctor for medical clearances before beginning any new exercise program. Inversion therapy may be better suited for your health, ask your doctor. Inversion therapy is basically hanging upside down to experience the benefits of reverse gravity. It helps drain the organs of stagnant fluids, increase blood flow to the head, neck and upper body while relieving the spine of pressure caused by the forces of gravity.

Caution: Shoulder pose may not be suitable for everyone at first. A "slant board" is a great beginner's tool, they are economical, less physically taxing and are an effective alternative, ask your doctor which would be best for you.

Ayurvedic Bow- Lay on belly, reach backwards, grab and hold ankles.

Cat Pose/Cow Pose

On all fours, lean forward and keep your knees on the ground, press your elbows close to your ribs as you slightly bend them, supporting the weight of your upper body with the triceps. This is similar to a push up. The toes are straight then flexed gripping the ground and the buttocks are tight supporting the lower back as you arch your mid back toward the ground and tilt your head upward looking into the sky.

Imagine a cat stretching forward and then reverse in a humping motion arching the upper back up toward the sky while dropping the head forward between the upper arms down toward the ground. The rhythmic pumping motion gets the organs and circulation flowing to stimulate metabolism. The alternating intervals that yoga produces, allows the muscle to utilize the hold and relax technique that is typical of stretching exercises.

Hatha Yoga

Hatha is a form of yoga, which involves deep breathing and deep belly laughter as a meditative practice. Forcing yourself to laugh out loudly. Doing this can be quite humorous especially if you can coerce a friend to try it with you. I bet the neighbors will wonder what you're up to. While sitting in yoga pose, think of something very funny to you. Start with a chuckle then crescendo with a roaring laughter keep your laughter going as long as possible and allow it to gradually exhaust you and subside. The effects are amazing. In addition, it is a fun exercise. Deep belly laughter works every muscle in your body and face. Real laughter can lower high blood pressure, decrease stress, decrease depression because of the release of feel good hormones such as Serotonin. It relieves pain by triggering a release of pain relieving agents and called endorphins.

Laughing Yoga

It has been said, "laughter is the best medicine". Laughing yoga exercise helps increase endorphins and feel good hormones that help offset depression. In laughing yoga we "laugh for no reason." Think of various comedic scenarios to jump start your laughter. Laughter is the best medicine so you can enjoy the health benefits associated with laughing yoga such as increased happiness and calmness and reduced stress and it also improves the level of energy and oxygen in the mind and body or work efficiency. Laughing is always a good feeling and it's one of the best kept secret anti-aging exercises for your face.

CHAPTER 9
Stretches & Warm Up Exercises

You must stretch and warm up before exercise as it helps prevent injuries. Once, you have stretched and warmed up your muscles. You are now ready to begin your three miracles Mind Body Exercise Routine. You may do either the morning or evening exercise routine of your choice, it is better if you rotate the routines to keep your exercise routine balanced.

Stretch & Warm Up Before Exercise

However, you must do at least one routine daily to lose weight. It is preferable that you do both. You will increase your rate and speed of weight loss by doing both and increase your fat and calorie burning potential.

Warm Up Exercises As Shown Above:

- Inner Thigh Lifts
- Buttock/Cellulite Back Leg Lifts
- Outer Thigh Leg Lifts
- Abdominal Crunches/Knee Lifts
- Leg Stretches
- Sitting Knees To Chest
- Elbow Buttock Lifts
- Floor Knee Lunge

Arm Exercise Basic arm exercises offer great fitness benefits and almost anyone can do them, even very young and older people.

- Hold your arms out from the side, horizontally.
- Bring your arms together touching the palms, pointing your hands flat.
- Stretch arms as far backwards as you can

Alternative:

- Row your arms in circles in a forward circular motion to the right and left sides.
- Reverse and Repeat.
- Row your arms in a counterclockwise circular motion.
- Repeat 10 times.

Hamstring Stretch–Bend forward at the waist while extending one foot forward while bending the opposite knee and while flexing your foot upwards at the ankle.

- Place both hands on top of the thigh just above the knee stretching the hamstring.
- Switch sides and repeat.

Hamstring Stretch

Hamstring Stretch

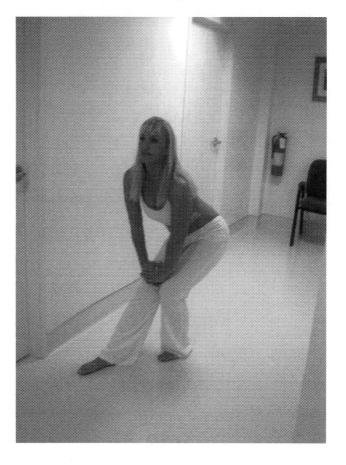

Quad Stretch-Balance yourself by holding the wall or a chair. Bend your knee lifting your foot off the ground behind you. Grasp your foot and pull back and up while lifting your foot to the sky behind you. This stretches your front thigh quadriceps. Switch sides and repeat.

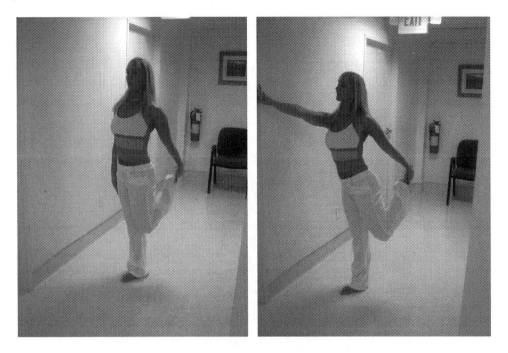

Quad Stretch

The larger front thigh muscles above your knee are a group of muscles known as your quadriceps. These muscles are large and support your body to run, jump and squat. Your quads need daily stretching because they are used so much and are important in your mobility. To stretch your quads follow the following instructions, as shown in the photos.

Make sure you have good balance when attempting to stand on one leg or either brace yourself against a sturdy chair or wall. Standing with both feet together:

- Bend knee lifting heel to buttocks.
- Hold ankle with cupped hand.
- Balance on 1 foot.
- Pull your foot and knee behind you.
- Maintain balance.
- Feel Front Quad Stretch.

- Hold for 3 seconds
- Switch sides and repeat.
- Relax.

Enjoy the feeling.
Repeat 3 Times.

Desk Stretches & Breathing Exercises

Chair Stretches Instructions:

- **Think Safety, First** – make sure you use a stable sturdy chair. The following are stretches are shown above from left to right:

  o **Head Tilt Neck Stretch**- tilt head to left or right until ear touches shoulder

- **Toso Stretch**- lift arms overhead, lock hands together, breathe deeply, tilt back to stretch.
- **Triceps And Shoulder Stretch**- bend elbow, over-head, touch hand on upper back, bend other elbow, reach up behind your back to lock hands.
- **Back Shoulder Stretch**- place hands together, behind your back, lift collapsed hands together upward toward the sky, forward bend at waist.
- **Side Body Stretch**- cross one leg over the other, lean forward, bending at the waist, lean forward, stretching arms to the opposite side, switch legs and repeat.
- **Lower Back Stretch**- feet flat to the floor, keeping spine straight, place palms on knees, lean forward.
- **Arm Hand Stretch-** lock fingers, invert palms, lift arms horizontal to your lap, shrug shoulders vertically then horizontally.
- **Right & Left Nostril Breathing/ Right/Left Brain Hemisphere Switching/ Brain Balancing Technique**- basically block the right nostril and breathe through your left nostril to relax. Basically, the left side of your brain controls the right side of your body and vise-versa, the right brain is your creative artistic side, your left brain is facts and numbers. If you are in a stressed out work environment this can be useful to calm stress and switch you from critical analytical brain mode to relaxed creative brain mode.

Additional Shoulder Stretch Instructions:

Sit or stand up straight in good posture.

- Bend your arm horizontally toward your opposite shoulder.
- Allow the posture to stretch your back shoulder blade muscles.
- Keeping your whole arm parallel to your shoulder height.
- Support your elbow with the opposite hand.
- Feel the back stretch.
- Hold the stretch for 3–5 seconds.
- Release.
- Switch Sides and Repeat
- Relax.
- Enjoy the feeling.
- Repeat 3 Times.

Triceps stretch– Bring your right arm above the head, bending at the elbow, touch your upper back with a flat hand, place your palm touching the upper back, with the opposite hand, grasp the elbow and gently pull toward the center of your body, behind the head, stretching out the triceps muscles of the upper arm. Switch sides and repeat.

Warm-Up Floor Exercises

Men's Floor Exercise Instructions:

- Think Safety, First– make sure you are on a non-skid surface with flat stable grounding. A yoga mat adds a protective barrier between you and the ground. Do a few of each in less than 15 minutes. As shown in the above photo collage listed from left to right in the collage as follows:
- Squat– bend at knees, shift weight to heels, never shift weight to toes to avoid knee stress.
- Kneel– kneel on one bended knee 3 times switch sides and repeat.
- Side Plank– lay on side, stiffen body and lift body on one forearm with palms on the floor.
- Hip Push-Up– Lay flat of back, knees together, thrust pelvis up toward the sky.
- Leg Lifts– From Hip Thrust Push Up position, lift and extend one foot at a time pointing toe upward
- Reclined Bicycle– lay on back lift feet into the air and peddle your legs as though your riding a bike

- Scissor Leg Lift Exercise- lay flat on back keep legs stiff and straight rotate lifting right and left legs in a scissor motion.
- Side Posture Leg Lifts- lay on the side with weight propped on elbow, lift your right leg laterally away from your left leg 10 times, switch sides and repeat.
- Elbow To Knee Ab Crunches- lay on your back do an abdominal crunch while bringing your right elbow to your left knee, rotate right and left sides.
- Supine Toe Touch- lay on back, lift feet into the air, reach your fingertips to your toes.
- Push-Up Leg Lifts- from push up pose, lift your leg off the floor behind you, switch legs and repeat.
- Hand & Knee Lifts- From an all fours position, extent your opposite leg and arm off the floor, switch sides and repeat.

Toe Touches- toe touches are one of the most common exercises that can be done, while standing, sitting or laying down. It is an important flexibility exercise because bending forward is a common movement in everyday life. Toe touching may help prevent the loss of mobility associated with aging.

Lower Back Stretches

Laying flat on your back, prop you weight onto your elbows. Point the toes and rock the weight of your legs outwards while you push yourself upward off the ground shifting weight to the hands & feet.

- Laying in fetal pose on your back.

  - Hold knees with arms.
  - Breathe.
  - Relax.
  - Repeat 3 times.

- Laying flat on your back

  - Knees bent
  - Feet Flat
  - Twist at the waist
  - Allow your knees to fall to your right side
  - Turn your head and neck to the opposite side of your lower trunk.
  - Feel the gentle stretch down your sides and into your lower back
  - Switch sides and repeat.

Side Bend Toe Touch

Sitting on the floor, spread your legs as far apart as possible, bend at the waist side ways until you touch the opposite foot with your hand, switch sides and repeat.

Spread Eagle

Lay flat on your back, stretch open arms and palms out to the sides, open legs and feet apart, breathe in deeply, hold and exhale slowly for 5 seconds, relax and repeat.

Reclined Bound Angle Pose Step-By-Step

Lie down comfortably on your back, with your legs extended and your arms at your sides, palms face up toward the ceiling. Bend your knees to bring the soles of your feet together and slide heels up toward buttocks and knees to right. The outer edges of your feet should be resting on the floor.

Bicycle Floor Exercise: Lay on your back propped up on your elbows. Extend one leg at a time in the air. Rotate right and left leg extensions as if you are pedaling a bicycle. This tightens abs as well.

Imaginary Bicycle Exercise Instructions:

Start, while laying face up on your back. You are basically pretending to ride an imaginary bike.

1. Bring knees back to the chest grasping arms around the knees.
2. Squeeze knees into chest, stretching the spine.
3. Extend knees and feet up from the chest into the air.
4. Place arms by each side, using your arms to balance and support your weight, place your hands flat on the floor on each side.
5. Raise feet in the air, while pushing down with hands on the floor, place your feet over head, as you shift your body weight to your shoulders, relax and stabilize your weight.
6. Slowly, bring your feet over your head and place your tip toes on the floor above your head as you lift your lower back off the floor. As the weight of your body shifts to your upper back and shoulders.
7. Bring your right or left leg into the air toward the ceiling, one leg and one foot at a time into the air. Take time to stabilize your weight onto your shoulders, using your arms to balance your weight, so that you don't fall.

Shoulder Stand (Sarvanga Pose)– helps relax the body and calm the mind as it aids in relieving stress and may help with depression. It also helps to improve mental clarity, memory loss and enhanced concentration. This pose helps provide a boost of dopamine and serotonin to enhance a sense of positive energy to your body, mind, and alleviate stressful emotions. Benefits accumulate over time with the regular practice of doing the Shoulder-stand yoga pose on a daily basis and in just a few minutes a day, it can help you feel refreshed and renewed every day and it's good for calming kids, too!

Once, you feel stable, bring the other leg up till both feet touch together in the air, with your body weight resting on your shoulders and upper back. You are now in Sarvanga pose.

Caution: Shoulder pose may not be suitable for everyone at first. A "slant board" is a great beginner's tool, they are economical, less physically taxing and are an effective alternative, ask your doctor which would be best for you.

Inversion Therapy Pose

The mother queen of all yoga poses is Sarvanga, it is a shoulder-stand pose that stretches the neck and shoulders, while toning the legs, buttocks, back, and abdominal core muscles. It is referred to as the "Queen of Asanas" because it provides many benefits to the mind and body, including:

- Inversion exercises increase the flow of blood to the brain.
- Inversion drains all organs and lungs of stagnant fluids.
- Stimulates thyroid and prostate gland functions
- Stimulates abdominal organs
- Improves digestion
- Drainage of excess phlegm and mucus
- Reduces fatigue and insomnia
- Relieves sinuses, asthma, sluggish metabolism and hormone imbalance

Beginner Slant Exercise

For some older, handicapped or obese people it may be a better option to use a naturally slanted surface with a gentle slope. A gently sloping hillside is the most natural option to reap the benefits of inversion therapy if this option is feasible it's worth trying.

This can be a fun activity for children, too. Try finding shapes in the clouds as an added stress reliever for children and adults may find it amusing, too.

- Outdoor grounding by laying upside down on a slanted surface, such as a grassy outdoor hillside, lay flat on your back, arms to the side, using hands on the ground to keep your balance. (not recommended on angles greater than 35-45 degree slant)
- The simple act of laying head down the hill is a form of natural inversion therapy, that helps drain stagnant fluids sitting in organs and to help increase blood flow to the brain.
- More advanced athletes may balance weight onto their shoulders, upper-back and arms.
- Use your arms to balance & support your body weight and hips.
- Raise and straighten your hips in the air feet on the ground knees pointing to the sky.
- Tuck your chin into your chest
- Rest the weight of your body on your shoulders and upper-back.
- Use caution to avoid flipping over backwards on a downward sloping hillside.

Modified Yoga Asana

Pelvic Push-Up & Head Lift Crunch – Choose a safe sturdy chair, lay flat on your back, knees bent, feet flat on the floor, push pelvis up toward the sky while keeping your shoulders, feet and hands on the floor, supporting your weight. Squeeze your buttocks tightly as you lift and then lower your pelvis back down, flat to the floor, lift your hands behind the head and crunch your abdominal muscles firmly as you raise your head toward your pelvis. Up and Down. Repeat 3 sets of 10 repetitions.

The Push Up

Push-ups build up your bicep muscles as well as your core strength, quickly. It can be difficult for a beginner to do one push-up much less ten. That's why it is the boot-camp choice as a disciplinary exercise for cadets. Push-ups are probably one of the most traditional exercises that build upper body and core strength.

Push Up Instructions:

- Lay on my stomach.
- Push body weight up with elbows & onto toes,
- Life then lower and lift your bodyweight up and down with your arms in an up and down motion.
- Repeat 10 Times.

Push Up

Push-ups are probably one of the most traditional exercises that build upper body and core strength and it's a great exercise for all the men and little men in the house but it's great for the girls, too!

Push Up Instructions:

- Lay on my stomach.
- Push body weight up with arms straightening elbows shifting weight onto hands & flexed toes
- Lift then lower and slowly repeat. Lift your bodyweight up and down with your arms in an up and down motion.
- Repeat as many times as you can work up to 10-50 Times depending on your endurance.
- Overtime strive to do more each time and you become stronger.

Alternate Hand Position for Push-Up To Work Various Arm Muscles

CHAPTER 10

The Three Anti-Aging
Mind-Body Exercises

As a person ages, they tend to lose flexibility and mobility. Therefore, one of the keys to anti-aging and longevity is stretching and exercise. These daily exercise practices can help you stay fit, flexible, mobile and healthier for extended longevity and a better quality of life. These mild exercises are beneficial in conditioning the major muscle groups. It is recommended for weight loss to do a daily minimum of 3 sets of 10 repetitions and gradually build up to 3 sets of 20 repetitions over time. Repetitions vary depending on the age and fragility of the individual. Older and more frail individuals should start with one set of 10 repetitions, and gradually work up to three sets of 10.

Healthy beginners should do 1 set of 15 repetitions and work their way up to 3 sets of 15 Healthy Individuals should do no less than 3 sets of 20 repetitions and work their way into more until the point of fatigue.

About The 3 Mind-Body One-Step Miracle Exercises

The Mind-Body Miracle Exercises consist of three ten-minute exercise routines that integrate yoga with traditional exercises to target all the major muscle groups in the body. These are designed to be safe and effective in healthy individuals. However, proper positioning is imperative to avoid strain and injury. It is recommended to seek counsel from your doctor or a qualified fitness trainer to ensure proper form and positioning. This powerfully effective exercise program is a combination of yoga and traditional exercises that are designed to be a quick, effective and easy way to tighten and tone your entire body, while working every major muscle group.

Mobility = Longevity

The 3 time-saving exercises that effectively tighten and tone every muscle group are in fact, integrative exercises that are combined with traditional exercise positions mixed with pilates and yoga positions. These 3 exercises were created by Joyce, the author as a certified fitness trainer for those people who did not have hours to spend in the gym so they could do their whole body in 30 minutes.

The 3 exercises are:

1. The Anti-Aging Mind-Body Core Builder.
2. The Anti-Aging Mind-Body Lunge.
3. The Anti-Aging Mind Body Squat.

Each exercise has these possible modifications:

- Beginner level
- Modified advanced level
- Body builder level with weights.

The following instructions are for the 3 exercises, invented to tighten, tone and strengthen every major muscle group in 30 minutes.

This portion of the Mind Body Exercise Program saves you time because it works multiple areas at once.

- The first exercise is a 3-step alternating abdominal core routine consisting of 3 core strengthening abdominal positions that you rotate the order on a weekly basis.
- You should never feel bored with your abdominal exercise routine. Switch your routine up on a daily or weekly basis to keep it working to improve your results.
- Rotate each of the following exercises each time you do your routine rotate these three abdominal exercises.
- Switching your abdominal exercises between these three routines will also keep your body responding and showing ongoing improvements instead of falling into a boring repetitive regimen that the body stops responding to.
- The following are the 3 exercises that you can do anywhere in just 15 minutes up to 3 x per day.

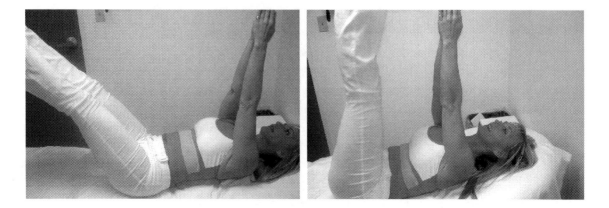

#1. Mind-Body Pilates Core Builder Exercise:

A.) **Mind–Body Flexion Extension-** I invented this exercise to simulate the benefits of pilates. This floor exercise works the abdominal, quadriceps, biceps and triceps all at once while increasing core strength.

- Lay flat on your back and assume the starting position by raising the legs and arms extending them up toward the sky while placing feet and hands in the air.
- Bend the knees caudad bend the arms cephalad and both parallel to the floor by bending arms at the elbow and bending legs at the knee.
- Keep your forearms and calves perpendicular to the floor, hold and flex the muscle contraction then lift the arms and legs straight in the air to the starting position and flex the muscles tight while extending legs and arms into the air.
- As your endurance and strength improves you may add weight. Use very light ankle & wrists weights.
- Repeat 3 sets of 10.

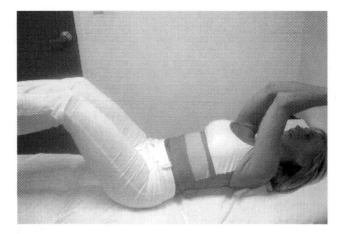

B.) **Mind-Body Side-Posture Sit Up-** this exercise provides a beautiful hour-glass or v-shaped body. It tightens and tones the abs, neck, along the jawline and decollete' area, arms and back.

- Starting position is lay flat on the floor, rock pelvis up to eliminate any space between the lower back and the floor.
- Cross your ankle over your opposite knee.
- Place your hands on the floor, the starting position bend your elbow into an L-shape with your arm, bent at the elbow hand on floor,
- Bending the knees and keeping the feet flat on the floor, cross the left foot over the right knee.
- Place the right hand on the back of the right side of the back of the upper back just below the head.
- Pushing up with the free left hand and arm brings the right elbow up to the left knee by doing a side posture-sit up while twisting the torso of your body and pulling it up at the same time using the abdominal muscles. Keeping your eyes on your elbow at all times as you touch the elbow to the opposite knee doing a side posture sit-up.
- In reverse of the previous motion, slowly return to the starting position and repeat this procedure 10 times each side.
- Switch sides and repeat the same procedure on the opposite side. After doing both sides, rotate sides and repeat 3 sets of 10 on each side.

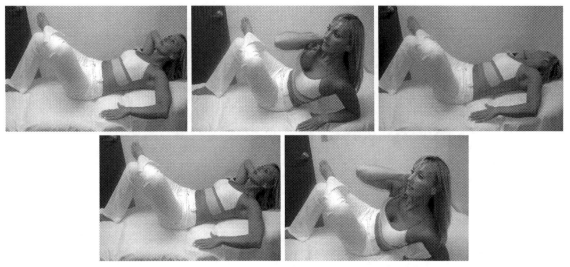

Side Posture Sit–Up

Alteration Scissor Legs Sit-Ups: instead of crossing your ankle over the opposite knee, keep knees together and touch your opposite elbow to your knee rotate between right and left knee. Switch sides and repeat

A

B

C

C.) **Lower Abdominal Crunch**-This is the most effective home exercise for lower abdominal muscles and is the only type of movement that will flatten the lower abdominal muscles.

Instructions for Lower Body Ab Crunch:

- Sit comfortably in a safe, supportive, hard chair.
- Sit on the edge of your chair, keeping your spine completely straight.
- Bring your knees up to your chest and
- Point your toes and slowly lower your feet back down to the floor
- Repeat 3 sets of 10 repetitions.

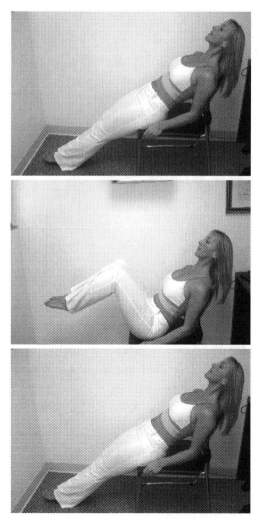

Lower Body Ab Crunch

#2. Mind-Body Lunges

Forward Launch/ Overhead Extension- standing with feet shoulder width apart, launch your right foot forward while bending down with the left knee as you move forward into a launch. As you are launching forward both right and left hands over your head and bring your hands together over your head in the air. Push your body back up into the starting standing position as you slowly lower your hand down to your side. Rotate between the right and left side. Repeat 3 sets of 10.

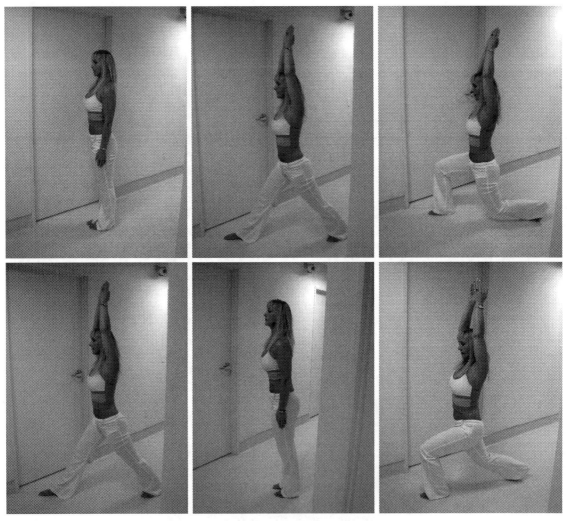

Anti-Aging Lunges
Switch sides and repeat 1 set of
10 work up to 3 sets of 10.

#3. Mind-Body Squat Warm-Up

A.) 2 warm-up postures to practice as a prerequisite to doing the Anti-Aging Squat to help improve your balance, before doing the 3rd exercise. However, once you master these two postures and good balance skills, you can skip this step and do the squat without this warm up introduction as you master the move.

Hands Overhead Chin-Up Heel-Lift (Feet Together)

These balancing postures help with improving balance and agility. Start with hands above the head, get a feel for your balance by practicing standing on your tiptoes with your palms together and hands in upward Namaste', looking up lifting your chin and dropping your head back while standing on the toes.

B.) **Toe Walking-** After you master the heel lift, supporting your weight on the ball of your feet, the next step is to practice the squat with your toes raised from the floor. Practice heel walking, too.

C.) **Heel Walking-** Place your hands on your upper thigh and squat while shifting all your weight to your heels, remember, your toes must be up off the floor. Once you have gained control of your balance, it's time to put the two parts together and do the integrated exercise, as follows.

Benefits of Squat Exercises

Humans have been squatting since the beginning of time. Hunter gatherers spent most of their lives in a squatting position collecting seeds, nuts and berries and squatting was even a survival posture hiding from predatory animals. Squatting exercises are useful today as squat exercises offer fitness benefits for both men and women and squatting doesn't require a lot of tools or space to perform, such as walking and running, the benefits are great. Squatting gives the body lower body strength. It is a common motion of early life and it's an ability we can lose with age if we don't stay in the habit of using this position. Doing repetitive squats is a common exercise amongst athletes but people of all ages can reap the rewards of practicing their squats. Squats are not only for weightlifters and bodybuilders. What makes squats the greatest exercise you can do is because its main benefits are that squats work most of the major muscles in the body in one movement, Squats build strength in the lower body, especially the buttocks, thighs, lower abdomen and back, and can help you build massive lower body muscle when you add weights.

- It is the number one exercise to see results quickly and is described as a quick exercise that leads to tightening and toning-up the body. Squatting helps us maintain our balance with age.

Muscles used in the squat:

The exercise is not limited to one muscle exercise, but many of the muscles of the body are used during this exercise, and the most basic muscles used in this exercise are:

- Gluteus Minimus & Maximus Muscles
- Quadriceps muscle
- Erector Spinae Muscle
- Stomach muscles
- Muscles of the knee
- Adductor muscles

Types of squats:

The squat exercise has several types, each with specific benefits.

- Chair Squats
- Always requires bending the knees.
- Always requires shifting weight to the heels to avoid knee injury.

- Calisthenics- Exercise may be done without weights.
- Weight Bearing- Exercise may be done with weights.
- Exercise may be done with jumping.

#3. The Anti-Aging & Mind Body Squat

#3 The "JOY SQUAT"

A modified, integrative, full-body squat exercise that works fast to tighten and tone your body, with noticeable fitness results within 3 days! It is the most complex of the 3 exercises that lifts and tones every muscle group. The "JOY SQUAT" is the one exercise that you can do anytime, anyplace and anywhere because squatting is an exercise that doesn't require a lot of tools or space to perform, like other exercises such as walking and running. This modified squat is the most simple and beneficial indoor exercise you can ever do for toning your whole body. It increases your sense of balance while producing incredible shape enhancing results. It works your:

- Quads,
- Hamstrings,
- Calves,
- Buttocks,
- Triceps,
- Biceps,
- Lower-face

- Neck
- Decollete
- Improves balance
- Mind–body connection

This integrative full-body squat works all the major muscles in the body all at once with one exercise, with added benefits such as:

- Elongates your spine
- Helps straighten your spine,
- Stretches Torso,
- Tones rib cage
- Tones Neck,
- Lifts up your chest/breast
- Lifts pectoralis muscles
- Lifts lower jaw-line and
- Simultaneously improves your overall posture.
- Strengthens your whole body.

1.)Feet Flat   2.) Heels Lifted   3.) Squat Heels

Joy Squat Instructions:

As you prepare to go into the integrative squat, make it your top priority to focus on taking pressure off of your knees. Shift your body weight to your heels as you jut your hips back as though you were sitting down in a chair. Watch your balance to avoid injury.

Weight is shifted to heels as you go deep into the squat, practicing with a chair under you is fine.

A.
- Stand straight, in mountain pose.
- Bend knees and squat.
- Lift toes while in the squat
- Bend elbows, working the triceps (may add wrist weights)
- Stand up straightening knees
- Lift heels
- Raise arms, with hands palms together over-head.
- Stretch torso & arms upwards to the sky
- Raise heels, shift your weight to the balls of your feet & toes.
- Repeat 10-30 times.

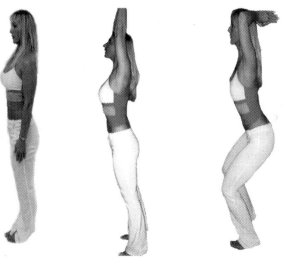

1.)Feet Flat   2.) Heels Lifted   3.) Squat Heels

Extra Body Mechanic Positional Tips:

As you bend your knees, lift your toes, as you squat, shift your weight to the back of your heels and raise your arms overhead and bend the elbows in a 45 degree angle. You can add wrist weights to work and define the triceps with this motion as it mimics a tricep kick-back.

Body Tightening Heel-Lift

A.)   Adding a "tightening" movement to the heel-lift increases the muscle tone and definition of your buttocks, calves, upper and outer thighs. As you perfect the posture you may add ankle weights. Tip-toe walking also tones the legs.

B.)   Stand straight with arms to the side, in mountain pose, or in attention then raise your arms and stretch extended arms toward the sky with palms together in upper namaste, while flexing your weight onto the balls of your feet.

C.)   For quicker muscle building results, you may add weight to your routine by using wrist and ankle weights or dumb bells according to your strength. Start with the lowest weight and gradually work your way up to higher weights.

D.)   Advanced "Jump For Joy" Squat Additions:

   Jump up from the squat as your endurance and strength increases. You can use a mini-tramp as your skills and balance improve. You can start doing jump squats without weights and you may add ankle or wrist weights once you master the technique.

The Mind Body "Joy Squat" Instructions:

- Starting on floor or mini-trampoline with your feet shoulder width apart,
- Bring arms up into upper Namaste' (palms together overhead)
- Looking upward, move chin upward, head dropped back, chin up.
- Bend the elbow backwards in a 90 degree angle, with forearms horizontal to the floor with the wrist, hands & palms touching together in bent overhead prayer pose into an upward triceps kickback with or without wrist-weights or dumbbells,
- Bend the knees, Lower the buttocks and the overhead wrist down toward the floor, lifting the toes and shifting weight onto heels
- As you squat, jutt the hips back as though you were going to sit in a chair, while keeping the toes off the floor and all weight on the heels, toes pointing straight ahead and toes up, off the floor. (this reduces stress on the knees and lower back)
- As you rise up out of the squat- thrust hips forward, raise wrist overhead in upward Namaste' pushing up with the forearms extending the diaphragm and torso forward stretching the torso and ribs upwards while lifting the chin, looking upward and dropping the head back.
- Chin up toward the sky elongating the upper body and spinal posture, with a straight spine.
- Shift weight standing up on the tip-toes while squeezing in thighs and buttocks and calves and reaching up toward the ceiling while clapping both hands together with fingertips pointing as far to the ceiling as you can reach.

- Raise from the squat position up on tiptoes as you raise your arms over head, straightening elbows and extending arms and hands into the air in a full body stretch and squeeze calves gastronomies as you do a heel lift, shift weight on tiptoes, flex & stretch. (See Demo Photos Below)
- REPEAT 3 sets of 10 repetitions.

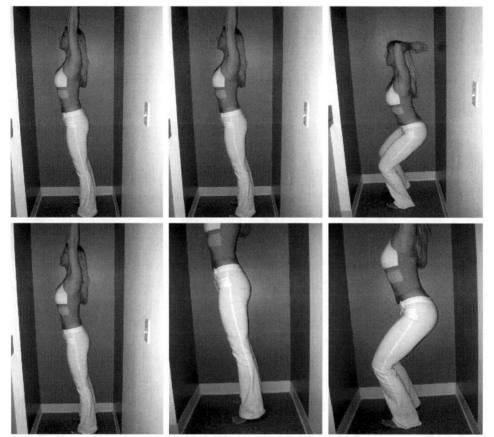

| 1.)Feet Flat | 2.) Heels Lifted | 3.) Squat Shift Weight To Heels |

Caution: To maintain balance and to avoid stress to the knees and low back, keep toes up and off the floor at all times while in the squat position and always shift your weight to the heels while in the squat position.

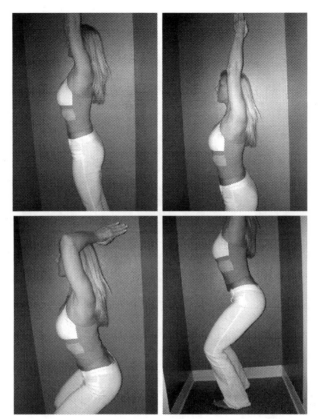

1.) Reach Up Heels Lifted 2.) Squat Shift Weight To Heels

Caution: To avoid injury keep the feet pointed forward and the ankles stable.

Chair Squats (alternative conditioning training)

When starting to exercise, some may not be ready to do the mind body squat but there is an exercise to help you improve balance by using a chair. For some, it is necessary to use a chair as a safety prop to help you stabilize your balance until you gain a steady balance and master the practice doing sets of squats and prepare doing sets of squats, without a chair. It's important to do a warm-up to avoid muscle tearing or injuries to the muscle. A warm-up is done for at least 5-10 minutes, prior to performing squat exercises, especially in the difficult exercises that require a high effort. Like a squat it's enough to improve balance and tone the lower body muscles and you only need a small space to exercise, you can add weights if it's desired to bulk up these muscles.

Bar Squats And Exercises Without Weights:

Exercise without weights is done to "tone" rather than "bulk-up" the muscle, rather to lean down and define muscles for more muscle definition without adding muscle mass. The goal is to add less weight but add more repetitions. Therefore, instead of doing 25 shoulder squats with 25 pounds of weight, you would do 50 squats with only the weight of the bar without added weights as follows:

- Stand upright while trying to separate the feet so that they are the same or more shoulder-level.
- To balance the position of the bar on your shoulders or overhead, while keeping your back straight, squat, shift your weight to the back of your heels. (not your toes)
- Shift back into the standing position, feet flat to the floor, by pushing the body up using the muscles of the quads and glutes, and push the bar overhead using triceps, biceps and forearms and the back to maintain balance.
- **Extra Balance Enhancing Technique:** Try a single squat in each set, it is done with the same steps for a normal squat exercise, but the descent is on only one leg while extending the other, resting weight on the back of the heel. This exercise is good for working the back muscles of the legs and buttocks, and to get rid of cellulite.

Advanced Toning Squats With Lite Weights:

Dumb-bell and barbell work doenst require much weight. Start with less weight and more repetitions to build tone and strength. After your muscles are strong add 5 additional pounds per week to build muscle and bulk up. These exercises are considered advanced or difficult, do not use more than 15 pounds in this program as the likelihood of an injury with improper technique is high.

- After the barbell is fitted with lite-weights, (no more than 15 pounds) the hands are placed on the bell just below level of the shoulders.
- Get under the barbell with slight bent knees and push up from the squat with the muscles of the legs
- The arm and shoulder muscles only balance the weight.
- The weight lifting comes from the legs only.
- Opening the feet slightly to the outside raising the toes to shift the weight to the heels.
- Start slowly in the sitting position
- Keep the back straight and continue to squat down until an "7" angle is formed between the knee, thigh and the leg.
- Rise up by pushing the body up with the back of your glutes, hamstrings and quad muscles.

1. YES   2. NO

Correct Body Mechanics Of Squats

- Do not squat on your tiptoes, this can cause knee injury. Shift weight to heels.
- Always shift your weight to your heels when squatting to avoid knee stress.

- While in a squat do not ever shift weight to your toes.
- Do not do heel-lifts while in a squatting position.
- You may do heel lifts in an upright standing position.

Benefits of Squats:

- Squats help tone the muscles of the lower body
- Pumps blood and lymph throughout the body
- Improves overall health
- Improves digestion and metabolism
- Increases blood flow and circulation
- Increases oxygen to all organs and vital areas of the body,
- Helps to get rid of cellulite
- Helps burn accumulated fat in the body
- Strengthens the muscles of the legs

Squatting exercises are resistance exercises that target the muscles of the legs and target the quadriceps and inner knee muscles to help increase their strength and protect knees to improve performance when doing other exercises. Squats exercises help get rid of waste in the body, and muscle movement during this exercise helps improve fluid flow in the body and facilitate the movement of waste inside the intestines, thus continuing to regularly extract waste outside the body.

Body Balance

Squat exercises help improve and maintain balance of the body, especially with age, as these exercises help strengthen the nerves that control the movement in the leg area, as well as be able to maintain the natural sense of balance that complements the functioning of fluid movement, as well as absorb Muscle behavior supremo techniques that are repeated during exercise.

Pre-exercise tips:

- Be careful to do some warm-up and prolonged exercises long enough to avoid damage.
- Be careful to use appropriate weights and avoid heavy weights at the beginning of exercise, which can be gradually increased with a trainer.
- Focus on good posture and back erection throughout the exercise to avoid any damage.

- If it is difficult to maintain good posture, it is good to use a corset or abdominal belt, or brace to protect the back and keep it upright.
- It is important to focus on the 60-70 degree drop angle between the ankles and the rear.

Prevention of Injuries Proper Squats Exercises:

There are a number of possible injuries in improper technique such as:

- Loss of balance
- Slipping is the result of loss of balance
- A strain of the muscles of the pelvis.
- Muscle tension in the muscles of the leg.
- Knee discomfort due to pressure from improper technique.

Women Natural Squatters

Women are natural squatters because women squat more often than men. It is a primitive exercise, hunter gatherers squatted in gathering fallen foods such as nuts and apples and in gardening and digging root vegetables such as beets, potatoes and carrots. Women are natural squatters as they squat often as they go through menstrual cycles, pregnancy, childbirth, and women tend to squat more than men when going to the bathroom when they urinate, too. Squat exercise should be done daily on a continual basis, as it is an integral part of daily life usually, Men can use squats as a sport alone or with weights and it is important for men to maintain their squatting ability with age, too. Squatting aids with consistent body functioning and it is the idea position for proper bowel movements and waste elimination. One of the most important exercises to maintain mobility, flexibility and a body that maintains a youthful tone is by making squatting exercise part of our daily lifestyle. You should be able to squat in a comfortable position throughout your whole life.

The Mind–Body 30-Minute Night Time
Anaerobic Exercise Routine

Take a deep breath and slowly exhale while in each position.

After becoming familiar with the routine, you may wear Wrist and Ankle Weights"
for the additional effect of weight bearing exercise. This will increase your results and the
effect of the exercises. Adding weights to your exercise routine, quickly reduces body fat,
adds more muscle definition and helps the body tone while producing lean muscle mass
and bone.

Warrior Pose:

Warrior Pose Lunges -

This exercise is a modified basic lunge with an integrated yoga warrior pose.

*   Lunge forward bringing hands in upward Namaste' as you
*   Lunge forward firmly on your right foot.
*   Look up tilting your chin and head upwards, palms together overhead then as you transition bring legs together at attention
*   Drop your arms back down to your sides as you transition to
*   Switch sides, lunge firmly on your left foot and
*   Look up tilting your chin and head upwards, palms together
*   Transition bringinging your legs together at attention
*   Repeat 10 times each side.

You will feel a greater stretch in the pectoralis and neck muscles which become shortened with age and technology posture. Looking upward is important in today's technology age for kids with their video games, adults with their cell phones and computers and for general improved neck and spine posture. Switch sides and repeat 10 times each side up to 3 sets of 10. with or without weights.

CHAPTER 11
Children's Exercise

Healthy Habits Start In Our Youth

Good exercise habits begin in our youth. Children are naturally full of energy and youthful vitality. Exercise is one of the best practices that can help children to vent pent up energy in a healthy way. The health of growing children is a priority in any parent's life, and few things are as important to a child's health is their level of exercise. Regular physical activity can help children and adolescents improve physical fitness, cardio health, respiratory fitness and self-esteem.

Lead Children To Exercise By Example

Child's 1ˢᵗ Breathing Exercise
In sitting position
Breath slow deep breaths.
Hold 3 seconds. Exhale Relax.
Enjoy the feeling.
Repeat 3 Times.

Exercise helps children build strong bones and muscles it also helps children to control their weight and helps reduce symptoms of anxiety and depression, lastly exercise helps improve strength, endurance and a stronger work ethic while reducing their risk of developing future health problems and health conditions such as:

- Stress/Anxiety
- Heart disease
- Diabetes
- Obesity

Youth Exercise

Exercise is just as important to our youth, as it is to adults. Kids naturally want to run and play so exercise can be used to help them expend some of that youthful energy and can help them develop healthier future fitness habits, for the next generation. Each person has an influence on those around them and caregivers are encouraged to share exercises with the children they care for. How you care for your own health and physical fitness is an important testimony to those you influence over. Children are especially impressionable and learn by example from the actions of the adults around them. We are the role models for the next generation and we influence the health and the future health of generations to come.

Floor Exercises & Yoga Poses For Kids- Children need exercise, too. It may be harder for children to shelter-in-place as they tend to be naturally more active than most adults. Hold each pose for three minutes. Then relax and repeat up to 3 times. Do stretches to warm up your muscles to avoid injuries, then you can do the 3 exercises tighten and tone every major muscle group.

KIDS YOGA
Prayer Pose
Shoulder Stand
Tree pose
Raised Hands Pose
Chair Pose
Extended Side Angle
Lunge Pose
Warrior 1 Pose
Warrior 2 Pose
Warrior 3 Pose
Plank Pose
Four Limbed Staff Pose
Zigzag Pose
Cobra Pose
Corp Pose
Boat Pose
Downward Facing Dog
Plow Pose
Standing Forward Bend Pose
Child Pose
Cow Pose
Cat Pose
Bow Pose
Camel Pose
Lotus Pose

(illustration to help children visualize the final poses)

Children's Exercise Games

- Fitness Video Games
- Hop Scotch
- Skipping Rope
- LeapFrog

- Jumping Jacks
- Hide and go seek
- Catch (any ball)
- Twister
- Chase

Fun Song & Dance Exercises For Children

You can always pop a dance cartoon video on the television or computer, but for those that wish to go the non-digital simple grass roots choice, the following are easy exercises for the youngest members of your family and the elderly, too. Also, older children can lead in the exercises as teachers to their younger siblings and family members and it is something elderly family members may get a kick out of doing, too. Always make exercise fun, laughter is the best medicine and laughing works your core muscles, too!

2-6 Years Old
Little Teapot

I'm a little teapot
short and stout!
here is my handle
here is my spout
When I get all steamed up
hear me shout,
tip me over,
and poor me out!

2-8 Years Old
Exercise & Song

Have the child say or sing the words and touch the body part for exercise:
Head & Shoulders, Knees & Toes
Knees & Toes
Knees & Toes
Head & Shoulders, Knees & Toes
Knees & Toes
Knees & Toes
Head & Shoulders, Knees & Toes

Physical Activities And School Athletics

Start your children in physical activities early in life, when their a toddle such as:

- Swimming Lessons
- T-Ball
- Soccer
- Dance Class
- Tap
- Ballet
- Hip-Hop
- Karate

C H A P T E R   1 2
Home Family Exercise Solutions

Family Exercise Benefits

Exercise has a lot of health benefits for the whole family. When families exercise together it results in a better connection among people. Those families who exercise together report a higher sense of satisfaction in their family relationships and this is even stronger for couples who exercise with their partners.

Family Exercise Solution

This is not only an Anti-Aging exercise plan, it is a Mind Body Exercise program that is suitable for adults and children of all ages. It is a quick and easy exercise program that tightens and tones every major muscle group while increasing flexibility. It is gentle and safe but effective making it a great exercise for the whole family and is designed to be done on a daily basis in ten minutes as part of your new Mind Body Lifestyle. It is a program that will help those in the sedentary category move into a healthier lifestyle that includes physical activity. The Mind Body Exercise program provides a quick and easy yet structured physical activity exercise routine that is safe and effective.

Healthy Family Lifestyle Changes

Having the desire for your family to make changes to their lifestyle to improve members of your families health for prevention of the development of illness is a good preventive idea. Each individual must want better health for themselves to make healthy lifestyle changes such as losing excess weight. However, it is completely acceptable to suggest someone get in better shape and better health when you have a desire that is genuinely based on concern for an unhealthy family member's state of health which poses a threat to their well-being. In fact, supporting a family member or partner in making healthy habit changes and living a healthier lifestyle together helps to promote a stronger family bond.

Home Family Fun Exercises And Other Gadgets

There are many options for exercise that can be done by the whole family, together, while at home. Exercise is a great tension and stress reliever that can be a fun activity to participate in for the whole family. Most of these exercises boost feel-good hormones, improve circulation and immunity and help tone muscles and increase flexibility. There are exercises that are also more specific for females and then those that are more specific to males. Regardless, the following are a few activities for everyone, some can be done indoors, others can be done in your yard and according to preference:

- **Family & Group Options:**
  - Floor Stretches & Exercises
  - Home band-weightlifting
  - Home gym workout
  - Neighborhood walks
  - Pilates bands
  - Limbo
  - Twister
  - Hula-Hoop
  - Jogging-In-Place
  - Jumping Jacks
  - Kick Ball
  - Badminton
  - Volleyball
  - BasketBall
  - Paddle Ball
  - Ping-Pong
  - Hide-N-Seek (smaller children)

- **Individual Home Exercise Options**
  - Floor Exercises
  - Chair Exercises

- Punching Bag/Kickboxing
- LED Light Juggling
- Baton Twirling
- LED's or Ribbon Stick
- Longevity Stick Exercises
- Exercise Pole
- Exercise Weights
- Bar Exercise
- Mini-Trampoline
- Hula-Hoop

The Family That Exercises Together, Stays Together

Couples Fitness Activities

Some activities can be done by couples. Studies show that couples who workout together stay strong and live longer, together. Working out with your romantic partner can help bring you both closer together and it can also mean better health and fitness results, increase longevity and harmony in your relationship.

Home Pilates Band Exercises

If you do not wish to bulk up with weights, you can tone and build muscle with resistance bands. All of your muscles need to tone is tension, adequate recovery, muscle adaptation, and progressive overload. Building muscle can be achieved with the bodyweight-only exercises such as with pilates or resistance bands. Additionally, adding resistance bands enhance the effects of traditional exercises, such as side leg lifts which aids in the toning of lower body muscles and buttocks shaping and lifting.

(Leg Lifts)

PHYSICAL ACTIVITY EXERCISE JOURNAL

	Mon	Tues	Wed	Thurs	Friday	Sat	Sunday
Date							
Time							
Type							
Goal							
Plan							

QUICK ANTI-AGING BASIC ROUTINE

Body Part	Exercise

Arms-   **Biceps curls**
                                                       Triceps cable

Shoulders-   **Overhead Press**
                                                       Lateral Raise

Chest-   **Barbell Bench Press**

                                                       Dumb bells Chest Press

Abdomen-   **Abdominal Oblique**

Side posture sit-up

Back-   **Cable Seated Row**
Hips & Lower body-   **Squats**
Back Leg Lifts

                                                       Side Leg Lifts
Legs-   **Stair Climber Calisthenics**

Weight Lifting Safety

Proper positioning is imperative, when using weights, there are a plethora of videos online to help you with positioning. Do three sets of ten exercises with minimum weight in the beginning and build up over time as muscle strength is gained.

Plank Poses

(Plank Pose/Push Up)

Push your weight up from your elbows through your arms and up on to your hands and toes.

- Straighten your knees and squeeze your buttocks, legs and ankles together.
- Hold strong for a few minutes.
- Release on your back down to the floor.
- Relax and Repeat.
- This pose can be done from anterior or reversed to posterior positions and even left or right side plank positions.

Kickboxing

Top Benefits of Kickboxing Workouts

Kickboxing is a good exercise for your total body fitness it improves your heart-health, joints, strength, balance, and coordination. Few exercise routines can outperform kickboxing for its benefits to your physical strength and improvement of your physical fitness plus it is a great way to burn calories and tame stress.

- Kicking and punching
- Tip- top shape
- Cardio fitness
- Burn Most Calories
- Reduce Stress.
- Is a high-energy exercise routine
- Boost confidence levels
- Improves Coordination
- Burns Massive Amounts Of Calories
- Ideal Cross-Training Workout
- Energy Boost
- Better Posture

Punching Bag Workout - The muscles in the arms, shoulders, chest, back, legs, and core are all engaged during a heavy punching bag training session, making it an effective full-body workout. With a heavy punching bag, you can practice punching the bag with the greatest possible force which, over time, improves your upper body strength and power. Power punching is a great way to build muscle in the shoulders, arms and back. By adding heavy body strikes and uppercuts, you can also target your pectoralis, biceps and traps, giving you a complete upper-body workout.

The Minimum Exercise For Fat Burning

Always keep in mind that in the first 20 minutes of moderate to intense exercise performance, muscle glycogen is used as the primary energy source and provides glucose for muscle fueling. It is important to exercise longer than 20 minutes to get into the most efficient fat burning phase of exercise. After this initial 20-minute phase of exercise, fatty acids and the branched chain amino acids are used as the major energy sources.

Pick An Activity That You Truly Enjoy Doing And Stick To It!

Complete Fit & Tone Home Workout Chart

You can do these exercises anywhere at any time and you don't need fancy gym equipment to do this exercise plan.

Complete Anti-Aging Workout

The Anti-Aging Exercise Plan by Joyce Peters, PhD

JUMPING JACKS
Jump For Joy!

LUNGES

SIT UPS

CRUNCHES

PLANK

SIDE PLANK

BEAR CRAWLS

BUTT KICKS

WALL SIT

PUSH UPS

SQUAT

DEAD BUG

BURPEES

POWER SKIPS

180 DEGREE TWISTING JUMP SQUATS

TOE TAPS

BICYCLES

FROG JUMPS

HIP CIRCLES

CLAMSHELL

FRONT KICKS

FLUTTER KICKS

KNEE PLANKS

CRAB WALKS

CRAB TOE TOUCHES

DUCK WALKS

PLANK SHOULDER TAPS

MOUNTAIN CLIMBERS

REVERSE CRUNCH

Dance

A timeless and fun activity that makes a great exercise is dance. Put on your favorite song and get down. Pick a dance style that you truly enjoy doing or take a dance class to learn a new style. Don't be afraid to try something new. Online dance classes are fun and there is a wide array of dance styles as follows:

- salsa,
- hip-hop,
- disco,
- tango,
- swing
- folk/clogging
- jazz
- ballet
- ballroom (which consist of 10 styles)

Choose the style of dance that you are most comfortable with that resonates with your natural rhythm and style. Any dance that keeps your feet moving and gets your circulation going will work as a great exercise practice that can help you stay fit for a lifetime. Get your dancing shoes on and do it for fitness and for fun. It is usually done in groups so therefore, it is inspiring and offers group support which is very motivating. Dancing burns off a lot of calories, slims the body beautifully and lifts the spirit.

Get A Pet That Requires Exercise

Caring for an animal requires exercise, after all we will walk a dog or ride a horse. Animals can help us produce hormones of loving and caring for our pets. Pets can make a great exercise companion.

Make Love

Intimacy requires the use of certain muscles and the human body is capable of enjoying sexual activity throughout a lifetime, including in older aged adults. Stay safe but sexually active if it is feasible throughout your lifespan. Sex keeps you looking, feeling and thinking youthfully. Sex burns calories and improves youthful hormone levels and an orgasm flexes and contracts every muscle in the body, also.

Kegel Exercises

The pelvic floor is a group of muscles that weaken with age, in both men and women and therefore, these muscles need exercise, too. In women, pelvic muscles surround the vagina and support other structures such as the uterus. In men, strong pelvic floor muscles provide bladder control and the contractions experienced in orgasms and in women these muscles support the labor and delivery process during childbirth. Pelvic floor fitness matters all throughout life. Over time, a woman's pelvic floor will weaken for a variety of reasons, including: Pregnancy and childbirth, high impact exercise, and even reduced muscle strength related to age. Like any other muscles, your pelvic floor muscles need to be worked out to maintain the strength you need.

Kegel Exercise Instructions:

- Locate your pelvic floor muscles and contract them by squeezing.
- Squeeze your pelvic floor as though you are cutting off the flow of urine mid stream.
- Contract your pelvic floor muscles for 3 to 5 seconds then release.
- Contract & Relax your pelvic floor muscles.
- Relax for 3 to 5 seconds in between each contraction.
- As your muscles become stronger, do a kegel push-up move. as you cut off the flow of urine pinch the muscle tight and lift it up inside your pelvic floor as high as you can by pulling the contraction upwards inside flexing the internal muscles upward toward your navel.
- For women, contract the kegel and until you feel it lifting your bladder and uterus.
- Add an additional step by squeezing in your lower abs while contracting your pelvic floor muscles to strengthen them all at the same time.
- For men, contract your pelvic floor to do a kegel and then squeeze tightly until you feel it lift your bladder, rectum and testicles as though you're drawing them up inside.
- Imagine your pelvic floor muscles shaped like two hammocks and flex the muscle from tip to end.
- Repeat the contract and relax a cycle 10 times.

You can do a kegel exercise anywhere, while you're driving in a car or riding on a bus, plane or train. You can add a kegel exercise to all 3 of the Anti-Aging exercises.

Mommy Makeover And Pregnancy Exercises

The following are the best exercises to do as a mommy makeover to get your pre-baby body back after pregnancy. However, these exercises are perfect for women, in general.

- tummy tuck sit-up
- butt-lift plank lifts.
- cellulite smoothing - back leg lifts
- pelvic tightening- butterfly leg fluttering.

Mommy Makeover Exercises

Caution: These exercises are only for postpartum women after your OBGYN doctor approves you to resume exercise and physical activities after childbirth.

Bladder Exercises

Stress incontinence is leakage experienced when you laugh, cough, sneeze, stand up, lift something or while doing heavy lifting or exercise. When the kegel muscles become weak, from aging or pregnancy, many people experience this type light bladder leakage because your pelvic floor muscles aren't strong enough to hold against the force being pushed against them. The pelvic floor muscles act as a hammock across the pelvis, holding the pelvic organs in place. When the pelvic floor muscles are strong, they prevent bladder leakage by applying pressure around the urethra. The good news is you can strengthen these muscles, too, with exercise.

Exercise And Aging

Exercise is important for everyone in the family of all age groups. Strength training has been shown to alleviate the symptoms of diabetes, osteoporosis, back pain, and depression, while helping you manage your weight. Strength training also contributes to a higher metabolism and enhanced glucose control.

Senior Stretching & Warm Up Exercises

Shoulder Tension Release

Stress can accumulate tension in the upper body. Shoulder rotation exercises can help to release tension in the shoulders, neck and upper back. These simple exercises can be done by most older people and young children and these exercises are good tension relievers for everyone of all ages, especially those who use computers, desk workers, video gamers and cell phone users.

- Rotate your shoulders in a circular motion clockwise 3 times.
- Reverse
- Rotate your shoulders counter-clockwise 3 times.
- Reverse and

Repeat 3-10 times, as long as it takes to relax.

Wrist & Ankle Rotation Exercises

Even if you are sitting behind a desk, on a computer typing or on a plane you can take 30 seconds to do these simple exercises as they stimulate blood flow and circulation which can be of great use for everyone especially older persons. It is recommended to do 5 minutes of wrist and ankle rotations for every 30 minutes of sitting. The benefits can even help prevent blood clots.

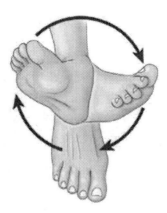

Rotation Exercises:

- Wrist
- Ankle
- Shoulder
- Neck
- Hip
- Fingers
- Toes

Hand Exercises

Most everyone can do simple hand exercises. Simple hand exercises can help you get in touch with your own energy force. You can also relieve stress or minor aches with your own healing touch. Touch increases hemoglobin and triggers the body's own natural healing processes. Many mind-body practices such as yoga, thai chi and Qigong, implement hand exercises.

Simple Hand Exercise:

- Bring hands together in a prayer position
- Rub your palms together quickly until you feel heat
- Create friction by rubbing your palms together until hot
- Touch the back of your neck or your temples with warm hands.
- Touch other areas of discomfort, feel the gentle heat
- Relax
- Enjoy the feeling
- Repeat

Imaginary Ball Rolling Exercise

Imagine a ball of warm light between your hands. Move your hands in a motion as though you were rolling the imaginary ball of energy between your hands. This is a good exercise for energy awareness. You can imagine a solid color of the ball or a rainbow of color. Focus on each color and what it brings to your mind. Stretch the ball into various other shapes in your mind. For example, you may visualize a ball of yellow light and stretch it into a banana in your mind.

Frailty Exercises

There are several exercises that are the best ways for seniors to strength train. Lite weight dumbbells allow seniors to isolate muscle groups to strengthen, while improving balance and flexibility. There are some exercises that are better suited for grandma's and grandpa's such as:

1. Wrist, Ankle and Arm Circles
2. Aqua walking or jogging (water exercises)
3. Air punching – front then to each side
4. Leg lifts- chair assisted
5. Pool ledge- in water push-ups
6. Arm curls- lite 1-2 lb. weights or water weights
7. A half-gallon of water weighs 4 pounds. You can lift it like a kettlebell to strengthen your arms.

The following exercises should probably be avoided if you're over the age of 65 or in frail health:

- Squats with dumbbells or weights
- Bench press
- Long-distance running
- Abdominal crunches
- Upright row
- Deadlift
- High-intensity interval training
- Rock climbing

CHAPTER 13

Face-Lift Exercises

Our face needs exercise, too. These are the 5 Anti-Aging Facial Exercises you can do that act as a facelift. It is just as important to exercise your facial muscles as it is the other muscles in the body, and even more so because our face makes many expressions throughout the day. If you are sad and angry all the time you're working those depressor muscles in your face that are detrimental to the uplifting muscles you use in your face associated with smiling and the moods and feelings associated with happiness and joy.

Smiling Is The Best
Lower Face-Lift Exercise

Therefore, if you are upset with things, situations or people in your life often, you must make a conscious effort to smile and avoid frowning no matter how you feel, you have the power to control how you react and the expressions you make as a reaction to negative feelings. If you can't control your facial expressions you may consider making environmental change to a happier environment which allows you to smile more or you may even make a choice to change the people you spend time with and spend more time with people who make you genuinely smile and laugh and who don't upset you.

Sad and negative expressions depress the (depressor-muscle) the natural angle of the mouth (anguli oris) and pull it slightly laterally. Thereby, it facilitates expressing sadness or when needed to assist in opening the mouth, the depressor-muscles are activated. Repetitive motion of frowning stretches these muscles and makes a permanent frown on your face while smiling all the time activates the lifting muscles and keeps them tone giving you a more lifted appearance on your face.

Exercising all the happy muscles in your face can help offset the effects of negative expressions. The following facial exercises stimulate and help lift all the layers of your facial muscles and help tone the skin, too. Facial exercises must be done correctly and by doing face exercises you increase blood circulation for a healthier glow as these exercises promote more oxygen and nutrients by increased blood flow which helps better nutrition utilization to reach the cells of the skin for a firmer, clearer complexion with a healthy glow. Start doing these exercises and you will begin to get that youthful lift and healthy glow on your face.

Peace-Sign Massage Exercises For Face

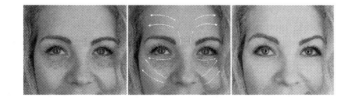

Exercise For Eyes: The W (Peace-Sign)

Helps Improve:

- Drooping eyelids,
- Crow's feet,
- Under eye bags and
- Puffiness.

Caution: always be gentle when touching your face during these exercises, it should always feel pleasant, never uncomfortable. Never press too deeply or too hard. Only use the pads of your fingertips avoiding skin contact with your fingernails.

Instructions: Avoid drag of the skin, always use a good quality facial oil or carrier oil as a lubricant. Avoid oils with artificial fragrances or preservatives, use an essential oil such as sweet almond or apricot oil as a lubricant. Our favorite is Royal Oil by Anti-Aging Skin Rx and Anti-Aging Brand.

Face Reflexology Exercise

Facial reflexology helps to eliminate toxins via points behind the muscle that aid lymphatic drainage, and relax tension in your face muscles. The movements work along the lymphatic points of the face, in turn reducing puffiness. It's also very soothing and relaxing to your facial muscles.

Face Muscle Acupressure Toning Exercise

Facial acupressure addresses toning muscles, energy balance and flow, specific point remedies, general wellness, skin tone and circulation. Many meridians and reflex zones run through the face so when you affect points on the face, you are affecting deeper layers of the facial muscles.

- Use the pads of your fingers on specific points
- The pressure will vary according to its location
- Apply enough pressure to activate the point
- Not so much pressure to cause discomfort
- Pressure varies according to your comfort level
- The only tools you need is your fingers
- Avoid contact of fingernails to skin
- Direction will start from top to bottom of face
- End with a warm wet cloth to remove residues
- Finish with a cold cloth compress to tone muscle.

Hot And Cold Contrast Face Compress Exercise

The contrast of the hot and cold alone helps tone your facial muscles. For maximum muscle stimulation it is always a good idea to start facial exercises with a warm compress to relax the muscles and afterwards apply a cold compress to contract, tighten and tone the facial muscles. Do not use extreme temperatures, never too hot or too cold.

Facial Exercise Pressure Points

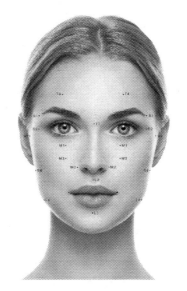

333 Face Rejuvenation Instructions:

The total time of this exercise is 3 minutes, each step.

- Apply Warm Cloth 3 Minutes To Relax Muscles,
- Gently Press Each Point 3 Times With The Pads Of Your Fingertips and Royal Oil For 3 Minutes
- Apply Cold Compress For 3 Minutes.

Cleanse away residues and follow up with moisturizer and makeup for the day or if at bedtime, apply your usual skin care regimen before your beauty rest.

Exercise Alternatives To: Botox and lid surgery.

Step 1

Make a peace sign or "v" sign. Gently press your middle finger together between your eyebrows and at the inner corner of the eyebrows, then with the index fingers, apply pressure to the outer corner of each eyebrow.

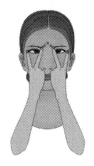

Step 2

Look to the ceiling, and lift the skin below the eyes upwards into a strong squint, and then relax.

Step 3

Repeat six more times and finish by squeezing eyes shut tightly without squinting for 10 seconds.

Step 4

**Anti-Aging Facial Exercises For
Under Eyes & Cheeks:**

Step 5

**Smile Line Smoother
Good for:**

- Cheek lines and sagging skin.
- Alternative to: Lower face lift and fillers.

Reverse Your Frown

The depressor labii inferioris muscle is a four-sided facial muscle located in the jaw area that draws the lower lip down and to the side.

Step 1

Make an 'O' shape with the mouth, hiding your teeth with your lips.

Step 2

Smile widely while keeping the teeth hidden and repeat 10 times.

Step 3

Next, hold the smile shape while placing one index finger on the chin. Then start to move the jaw up and down as the head tilts gently back. Relax and repeat twice more.

Anti-Aging Facial Yoga For Forehead:

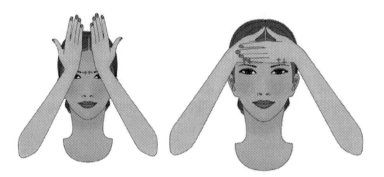

- Smooth The Brow

Good For:

- Horizontal forehead lines.
- Alternative To Toxin Injection

Step 1

Place both hands on the forehead facing inwards and spread all of the fingers out between the eyebrows and hairline.

Step 2

Gently sweep the fingers outwards across the forehead, applying light pressure to tighten the skin.

Step 3

Relax and repeat 10 times.

Anti-Aging Facial Exercise For Brows:

- Flirting Eye Exercise

Good For:

- Deep eye hollows and drooping eyebrows.
- Alternative To: Eyebrow lift.

Step 1

Lift your eyebrows as if you were flirting with someone.

Step 2

Lower your eyebrows to their normal position

Step 3

Repeat 10 times. Do up to 3 sets of 10.

Step 4

(Optional) place hands, lightly over brows to add weight resistance to your exercise, raise brows and repeat steps 1, 2 and 3.

Anti-Aging Kiss The Sky Exercise For Neck:

- Good For: Lines and loose skin on the neck.
- Alternative/PreventiveTo: Neck or jowl lift.

Step 1

Looking straight ahead, place the finger tips at the bottom of the neck and lightly stroke the skin downwards with the head tilted back.

Step 2

Bring the head back down to the chest and repeat twice more.

Step 3

Finally, jut the lower lip out as far as possible to pull the corners of the mouth down. Place your fingertips on the collarbone with the chin pointed upwards. Hold for four deep breaths.

Facial Lymphatic Drainage

Hook your first two fingers of each hand above the collar bone and gently press in a pumping motion ten pumps daily, this helps:

- puffy eyes and lids
- eye bags under eyes
- dark circles under eyes
- swelling in the face
- bloating in the face

Microcurrent Mimics Face & Body Exercise

Microcurrent uses electrical currents to flex and tone the muscles with impulses rather than manual repetition exercises. Microcurrent facials do the same thing to your face, you may use a home facial device without paying a facialist to do it for you, though it is nice to have a professional facial, too. Today, most women do many of their own treatments at home. One option for home use is the Anti-Aging Beauty Wand Kit and it's important to use good skin care too, such as Anti-Aging Skin Rx by Anti Aging Brand. It is a good home facial lift option. You can purchase a starter kit of both on ebay it includes the beauty wand and a starter size skin care kit.

C H A P T E R   1 4

Water Exercises

Hydration Water Therapy Exercises

Everyone knows about the importance of water for good health and good hygiene practices. It's important to wash our hands frequently and bathe or shower daily. This helps prevent risk of infectious conditions and water has a calming, soothing effect in many ways. Additionally, water offers stress relieving benefits as well. Water is cleansing, refreshing, relaxing, revitalising and invigorating, depending on the temperature or flow of the water you are submersed in. A bath can calm you down, a cold water-fall can invigorate you.

Water Sports Are Important Exercises

Mermaid Tail Kicks- Targets Abs and Legs - Summer Perry

A. Tread water in the deep end of the pool, arms out to sides and legs together extended beneath you.

B. Engage abs, squeeze legs together and sweep them backward, bending knees slightly, then quickly extend them forward (like a dolphin or mermaid tail). Counter balance motion by sweeping arms through water in the opposite direction of legs.

C. Continue for 1 minute. Your whole body should initiate the movement from your core then through your legs.

Exercise Drinking Enough Water

Drinking water is also an important part of life as our body's are over 70% water. Water is H2O hydrogen and oxygen. So we not only get oxygen from the air we breath we get it from water. Oxygen is a nutrient the brain and heart need constant flow of oxygen to prevent damage. As you exercise more, drink adequate amounts of water, daily and enjoy the benefits of water for your good-health.

In Water Pool Exercises

Water aerobics and water exercises take pressure off your joints and make movements easier without the full weight of gravity. Additionally, there are added health benefits as contrast baths are especially good for better health and healthy aging. In water, exercises offer added resistance training as you go through the motions and positions which simulates the effects and benefits of light weight bearing exercise without the joint stress.

Switching between hot and cold water stimulates many natural healing mechanisms within the body. Finish off every shower or bath with a cool water rinse and the colder you can tolerate it the better for toning the tissues over time it helps keep your body firmer. Exfoliating and Body brushing also helps with cell renewal and circulation and are a healthy hygiene exercise to include in your daily self-care routine.

Water Therapies Calm The Mind & Body

3 Minute Mind Calming Water Exercise

Think of the beauty of nature, a gentle stream, a beautiful beach, a field of wildflowers with a flowing stream, if you can go take a walk in a place like this, even better, but if not you can always go there in your mind and the calming effects are similar according to brain scientists. For those who can't venture outdoors you can calm your mind anywhere, anyplace and anytime by simply doing the following.

Sit in a quiet and comfortable place. Put one of your hands on your chest and the other on your stomach.

1. Close your eyes, visualize the water flowing over you and through your body cleansing away all stress and anxiety.
2. Begin to relax by breathing
3. Inhale- Take long slow deep breaths and regular breath in through your nose.
4. Exhale- Breathe out through your mouth, slowly and completely.

5. Calm your mind, take your thoughts off of daily life and imagine yourself in a tranquil place.
6. Repeat this process at least 10 times or until you begin to feel stress and anxiety subside.

Think of nature, a gentle stream, a beautiful beach, a field of wildflowers, if you can go take a place like this, even better but if not you can always go there in your mind and the calming effects are similar according to brain scientists.

Bathtub Crunches & Sit Ups

When you are bathing take the time to do a few sets of crunches while washing your hair and rinsing and applying conditioner and rinsing. As you lay back to wet your scalp focus on your abdominal muscles doing all the work. Crunch you abs as you lather up. Do a few sit ups between the rinse and repeat crunches.

Spa or Pool Floating Exercise

Floating in water increases your mind body connection as you must focus on controlled breathing, inhaling enough air in your lungs to float and letting your muscles relax enough that your body can float. Floating is the ultimate mind-body exercise.

C H A P T E R   1 5

Brain & Organ Exercises

When you exercise you are not only improving the muscles you see but also you are improving the health of some muscles that you can't see, which are located in your interior body. Exercise increases the oxygen absorption to your brain, heart and lungs as you breathe in more oxygen and exhale more carbonic acid waste to improve the health of not only your muscles but also your organs and entire body.

Exercise improves the health of your entire body, including your internal organs systems also exercise decreases stored fat which improves cardiovascular health and reduces cardiovascular stress and risk factors by reducing stored fat you improve your heart health and improve the oxygen to your brain and muscles.

Age Related Brain Fitness and Exercises

Declining brain health and memory loss are not inevitable parts of aging! You can be mentally sharp and maintain your ability to learn, reason, and remember into old age by eating right, exercising your mind and body, getting enough sleep, managing stress, connecting with others, and challenging your brain.

Your Brain's Role In Exercise

Your brain is an organ which requires exercise, too., The brain is the most complex and fascinating one because it plays a role in every function of the human body. Your brain controls many other organs and all of our thoughts, memories, speech including every movement you make during exercise.

"I used to think the brain was the most incredible organ in the human body, but then, I remembered the organ that was making me think that"...

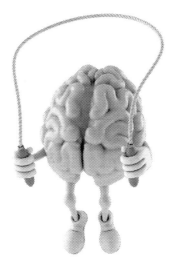

Everything You Believe, Think & Do, It All Starts In Your Head

Thoughts Self-Image

There is power in how you perceive yourself. there is power in how you think about yourself. Your thoughts are powerful in creating your image, including your body image.

"Your words become your actions,
Your actions become your habits,
Your habits become your values,
Your values become your destiny." — Gandhi

Everything You Do, Begins Within The Space Of The 8" Between Your Temples, Your Brain.

Neuroscience

Your brain is not a muscle but it is the first body part you activate to move every muscle you have to exercise. In fact, your brain is most fat, so the stuff you want to keep from accumulating on your body. Your brain is the fattiest organ in your body and at 60% fat, good dietary fats, such as omega-3s and omega-6s, are vital for brain and body health. Even though we're told to treat our brain like a muscle and exercise it, the brain isn't actually a muscle. While your brain may not be a muscle, as many believe, you still need to exercise it as you do the rest of your body to help keep it healthy and functioning at its best.

- Read & Recall Exercise- Reading is an activity that boosts cognitive skills and enhances lost vocabulary, reading can help reduce feelings of isolation for anyone anywhere anytime.
- Memory exercises become more important with age. You can help elderly family members enhance their memory by asking your older loved one to retell the story of their life or to tell you about a story they read once.
- Reading and storytelling is a brain exercise that helps us develop sharper memory skills.
- A good recall memory exercise is to read a chapter in a book then give a summary of the chapter they have finished each chapter in the book. This also helps increase social interactions with others which is also important with elderly.
- Practice happy outcome storytelling.
- Sing songs, it stimulates your brain to remember the words and tones.
- Repeat the lyrics and do a voice scale of the musical notes, tones and sounds.
- High blood sugar is linked to memory loss
- Your diet and exercise practices can help you fight against the brain changes linked to dementia and Alzheimer's disease
- Deep sleep may help wash away beta-amyloid plaques linked to Alzheimer's disease
- Certain exercise lower your risk of dementia and helps boosts new neuron development
- Eat a brain-boosting diet, eat more good fats and avoid processed sugar.
- Do exercises that help improve cognitive fitness
- Drink camomile tea before bed to improve sleep
- Do deep breathing techniques to manage stress
- Stay socially active
- Do activities to challenge your brain such as puzzles and games
- Younger teens may prefer VR and video games

- Children and elderly can name things you can wear on your feet that start with the letter "s"
- Play trivia games, checkers, dominos, cards, board games, ect.
- Name an object for every alphabet in your name. Over time, work up to naming 3 or more objects or words that start with each letter of your name, try using different words each time.
- Take a course, learn something, new.
- Pick a new topic to study.
- Exercise your brain and keep your mind active, too.

Exercise In Laughter- Keeping A Good Attitude And Sense of Humor With Age

Let us not forget about the elderly. Most of the oldest living people have outlived everyone they know. This can cause loneliness, sadness and depression. That is why it is important to be aware of those around you who may be in need of a kind word. Make a point to reach out to those you may recognise as a loner in your community. You can use the opportunity as a growing and learning exercise. You can learn alot from these individuals. For example, while interviewing some of the oldest people on the planet I've come to realize most of them have an incredible sense of humor and seem to be able to see a silver lining in regards to their present situation.

Not only do they usually have a sense of humor but they usually have an extraordinary sense of humor. Being able to stay light hearted and to still be able to be fascinated by life and interested in finding joy in life. Having an inquisitive mindset and finding ways to continue in being amazed by the wonders of the world. Staying in touch with current generation is important and other notable factors about their life are:

- Most have a good attitude and outlook on life.
- Most had good relationship skills.
- Most kept physically active
- Most are not over indulgent in anything
- Most avoided over eating throughout their life.
- Most stay active and get some form of exercise.
- Most were not worriers, they were warriors of life.
- Most loved deeply and laughed often.
- Most found things to keep themselves busy and amused.
- Most accepted age and the idea of growing older, gracefully.
- All said they enjoyed being socially active rather than being loner types.

Overall the oldest living people seem to be able to feel fondly of their life even if they had times of hardship they had a tendency to keep a positive mindset and find the silver lining in most situations.

Attitude is 90% and Circumstance is 10%

Organ Exercises

A muscular organ is a group of muscular tissues that work together to perform specific functions. Many internal organs have a muscular action that requires exercise, too. Peristaltic action is a muscular contraction that pushes your food through your alimentary system during digestion all the way from your mouth through twenty feet of intestines until elimination results in the toilet.

Heart Exercise

Your heart is a muscular organ and every time you do cardio you're doing heart exercises. In the case of your heart, as an organ, it's function is to pump blood 24/7 throughout your body from birth till death, non-stop. Additionally, the heart is largely made up of a type of muscle tissue called cardiac muscle. When this muscle malfunctions it can cause a heart-attack and when this muscle stops beating life ceases. Every Time you do physical exercise, you also exercise your heart. Heart nutrition is extremely important, too. Your heart needs good fats and avoid artery clogging bad fats. Also, your heart needs minerals like, magnesium, potassium and calcium to keep the muscle healthy and functioning properly. It functions as a bio-electric mechanism and like a battery is made of acids and alkali in a copper top cylinder filled with zinc this combination of chemistry sustains the bioelectric impulses for your heart to beat throughout a long lifetime.

- It's not about how much good fat your eating
- Your body needs good fats.
- It's about not eating bad fats
- Not eating bad carbs.
- Avoid bad carbs-
  - Cakes
  - Cookies
  - Sugary energy drinks
  - Pasta
  - Bread

- Eat good fats-
  - Avocados
  - Fish
  - Eggs
  - Protein- Hemp or plant protein
  - Evening Primrose Oil (if vegan)

Exercise To The Body Is What Reading Is To The Brain

C H A P T E R   1 6
Exercise Diet Nutrition Tips

Diet & Nutrition Tips

Good nutrition is important. Our body needs the daily recommended allowance of nutrients to function properly and for hunger to be satisfied. Additionally, our body requires a daily intake of adequate amounts of water, typically, our body weight, divided in half equals the number of ounces of water we need to drink in a day. In times of stress, we produce adrenaline and other harmful stress hormones causing a need for extra nutrition, as stress burns up B vitamins and depletes our adrenals which can cause us to crave carbs and sugar for fuel while slowing down our metabolism and causing our body to store more fat.

Collagen Protein

Collagen is a protein that is necessary to keep your muscles strong and functioning properly. Collagen is important for the health of your bones, skin, ligaments, and tendons and studies show that collagen supplements help boost muscle mass, also when blended with hemp or whey protein. The most important nutritional addition you can make to your diet that will aid your body as a preparation for exercise is a protein supplement such as a collagen protein supplement. The combination of collagen's high bioavailability with its high amino acid content makes it optimal post-exercise nutrition that rapidly absorbs and can quickly work to help repair and replenish proteins broken down during exercise. Collagen Peptides have been proven to help with weight loss and reducing body fat, too Collagen can help you build lean muscle, aid weight loss, and improve your skin texture.

Additionally, collagen peptides help reduce inflammation and improve digestive and GI health. Try Anti-Aging Brand Collagen.

Up To 10% of Muscle Tissue is Composed of Collagen

Eat Specific Foods To Boost Your Metabolism

Eat protein-rich foods, such as meat, fish, eggs, dairy, legumes, nuts and seeds, which help increase your metabolism for a few hours. Such as:

1. Tea/ Green Tea (contains protein and aminos)
2. Proteins
3. Iron Rich Foods.
4. Chili Peppers.
5. Coffee.
6. Legumes and Beans
7. Metabolism-Boosting Spices
8. Cacao

Make Some Better Diet And Lifestyle Choices:

These are some choices you will be faced with.

- Watch TV another hour or <u>take a 30 minute walk?</u>
- Eat a cookie or <u>eat a piece of dark chocolate?</u>
- Have a candybar or <u>have a protein bar?</u>
- Drink a soda or <u>drink a protein shake?</u>
- Eat the bad carbs <u>or eat the good salad carbs?</u>
- Eat hydrogenated snack chips or eat <u>nori seaweed?</u>

A diet rich in plant protein and amino-acids and good fats will help with cravings because your diet can provide the building blocks for muscle. For example, one cup cooked quinoa provides about eight grams of protein and five grams of fiber. Unlike some plant proteins , quinoa is a complete protein , and it contains all nine essential amino acids that our bodies cannot make on their own that must be consumed in your diet.

Exercise Protein And Nutrients For Mind & Body

The age old myth that athletes need to eat meat for protein has been disproven. You can get plenty of proteins from plants, too. Research has shown that all plants contain protein and at least 14% of the total calories of every plant is protein. For example, broccoli contains more protein per calorie than steak and spinach is about equal to chicken and fish per caloric intake. Additionally, there is a newly discovered toxin formed by the metabolism of the amino acid carnitine when we eat meat called trimethylamine oxide (TMAO). When we eat red meat, the carnitine interacts with our gut bacteria, forming trimethylamine, which is then metabolized by the liver into TMAO and studies show it may lead to heart attack, stroke, and death. Also, TMAO reduces our body's ability to excrete cholesterol.

Protein Muscle Fuel

Believe it or not, some plants contain more protein than meat! Plants have taken a bad rap as not being enough protein for a bodybuilder and it's not true! Infact, broccoli has as much protein per calorie as red meat and spinach has an equal amount as fish or chicken calorie per calorie! Meaning you can eat a bulk of protein and fiber filling veggies per a serving of meat and the veggie proteins will give you more of an abundant variety of other nutrients, antioxidants and phytonutrients making certain veggies a superior choice in comparison to meat alone. The following are examples of vegetables that have as much protein as meat not to mention the other nutrients they provide giving more balanced nutrition than meat alone:

- Seitan- concentrated wheat gluten like tofu
- Pulses-Tofu, Tempeh and Edamame
- Lentils
- Chickpeas
- Beans
- Nutritional Yeast
- Hemp Seeds
- Green Peas/English Peas

Want A Beef Steak? Try A Beet Steak!

Beets are packed with essential nutrients. Beetroots are a great source of protein, fiber, folate (vitamin B9), manganese, potassium, iron, and vitamin C. Beetroots and beetroot juice have been associated with numerous health benefits, including improved oxygenated blood flow and increased exercise performance. Beets are rich in natural compounds called nitrates. Through a chain reaction, your body changes nitrates into nitric oxide (NO), which helps oxygen flow to the muscles to give you that pumped look when pumping weights. Also, it improves blood flow and blood pressure. Beet juice may boost stamina, improve blood flow, and help cleanse and build the blood. You can add a spoon of chia seeds or sesame seeds to add more protein to your dish.

Beet-Steak Recipe

- 2-Large Red Beets- sliced thick ½-¾ inch
- 1- Tablespoon Coconut Oil -
- 1- Tablespoon Sesame Seeds or chia seeds
- 1- Slice Of Onion or 1 Tablespoon of Chives
- ¼ Cup of Water

Cooking Instructions: Melt the coconut oil in skillet and saute the beet-steaks and sesame seeds till covered in oil. Add onions or chives over beets. Add ¼ of water, sizzle and simmer, cover and cook until water evaporates and beets caramelize turning once. Serve with a side of salad Asparagus or Brussel Sprouts. Enjoy!

Nutrition Facts Beets

Calories: 44 per large beet (about size of your fist)
Protein: 1.7 grams
Fat: 0.2 grams
Fiber: 2 grams
Vitamin C: 6% RDI
Folate: 20% RDI
Vitamin B6: 3% RDI
Magnesium: 6% RDI
Potassium: 9% RDI
Phosphorous: 4% RDI
Manganese: 16% RDI
Iron: 4% RDI

Want A Burger? Try Mushrooms!

Mushrooms are relatively high in protein, averaging about 20% of their dried mass in protein alone plus portobello mushrooms have a thick meaty texture similar to beef when cooked. All mushrooms contain a wide variety of essential amino acids and they are low in fat (0.3 – 2.0%), high in fiber and provide several groups of vitamins, particularly thiamine, riboflavin, niacin, biotin and even vitamin c, ascorbic acid. When you grill a big portobello mushroom top it can be as filling and satisfying as a meat burger and may satisfy your appetite even better than mean because of all of the additional nutritional value mushrooms have to offer. Mushrooms provide protein energy, anti-aging benefits for skin and even boost your immune system, too! Some types of mushrooms are known as "magic-mushrooms" and they have long received a bad rap for being toxic, psychedelic or poisonous so stay away from those varieties and only buy edibles from a trusted seller, never harvest them yourself unless you are a mushroom expert. There are a variety of food grade mushrooms that are not psychedelic, toxic or poisonous and they offer extraordinary health benefits.

Ways to consume mushrooms:

- As a tea
- Raw (as a snack)
- In salads
- Grilled as a main course
- Stuffed, baked, broiled, or sauteed'
- Added to most any dish

Mushrooms have a very meaty flavor but it isn't an indication that they are equal to meat in comparison to their protein content. Mushrooms contain protein but are not a substitute for meat nutritionally because they are not equivalent in protein but they can curb your appetite for meat as a meat alternative because of their meaty texture.

Too Much Animal Protein Can Harm Your Health

Meat and animal proteins produce acid ash residues in the body chemistry. When we overdose of animal proteins it creates a biochemical imbalance that can block the absorption of other essential nutrients. There is no doubt that meat provides a lot of protein but too much can be almost toxic so don't feel like you must eat meat to build muscle because beans, eggs, nuts, yogurt and even broccoli give you a lot of protein, too! The following non-meat foods contain plenty of protein:

- Nuts and seeds (4–10 grams per 1 ounce serving):
    - Walnuts,
    - Cashews,
    - Pumpkin seeds,
    - Pistachios,
    - Sunflower seeds,
    - Almond butter,
    - Hemp seeds
    - Chia seeds
    - Flax seeds.

AntiOxidants Post Workout Recovery Foods

Moreover, antioxidants are important for good health in exercise recovery and antioxidant levels are sixty times greater in plants than in meat. In fact, even iceberg lettuce offers more antioxidants than salmon. Plants also help balance the body chemistry. Therefore, the body metabolises plants better than animal products and consuming at least half of your diet in plants is the best diet for a health balance. Plants are the most important part of your diet and plant based food are important for a healthy body during exercise, too.

CHAPTER 17

Stress, Relaxation and Sleep Exercises

Stress is known as the silent killer. If you feel like you are juggling more than you can handle, it is time to start doing stress management exercises. Often people cite their work or job as being the source of their stress. High stress causes fatigue and leaves a person feeling exhausted and not feeling like doing exercise but that is when we need exercise the most. People with high stress benefit greatly from doing stress relieving exercises.

Stress Relieving Exercises

Try doing some simple but powerful stress relieving techniques For example, taking long, slow, deep breaths also known as abdominal or belly breathing.

- Stress Ball Therapy-
    - squeeze a stress ball to release stressed energy

- Breathwork Meditation- Body Relaxation Scan-
    - This technique blends deep breathing with focus on each body part as you lay flat on your back, with intent to relax all muscles one by one head to toe.

- Guided imagery-
    - Visualize yourself in a relaxing place.

- Mindfulness meditation
    - be mindful of your breathing, and thinking peaceful calming thoughts

- Yoga, tai chi, and qigong
    - slow gentle movements to calm and destress

- Repetitive prayer
    - praying for peace and tranquility and having faith that god will provide peace to you.

Mind-Body Stress Reduction Exercises

Mind-Body Exercises can be done anywhere, in any small space. Yoga is a combination of stress relieving mind-body exercises that originated in India thousands of years ago that is still practiced by many people, today. The original vedic yoga involved posture, breathing, meditation and healthy living.

Foods To Naturally Calm Stress & Relax Muscles

Tryptophan is an amino acid that is known as nature's natural valium, of course it is non-addictive, safe and is found naturally, in some of the foods we eat.
Tryptophan containing food such as:

- Turkey
- Skim Milk
- Parmesan Cheese

Magnesium rich foods:

- Almonds
- Spinach
- Cashews
- Pumpkin seeds
- Peanuts

Magnesium helps stop muscle spasms and cramps by helping to relax muscles and may help with brain functions that reduce mental stress and tension, too.

Cacao And Dark Chocolate

Chocolate has a high tryptophan content, tryptophan a calming amino-acid that is also found in turkey that gives us that relaxed feeling after eating thanksgiving turkey. So if you're a vegan or vegetarian chocolate is another way to get a dose of calming tryptophan which the body uses to turn into mood-enhancing neurotransmitters, such as serotonin in the brain. Try to use a daily square of dark chocolate over taking a chill-pill, a daily chocolate habit would be a much better option in the long run because it doesn't block your emotions or leave you feeling like a spaced out airhead all numbed up so that you feel you can't move off the sofa, muchless exercise. Nobody wants to feel like a zombie in the apocalypse. We all want to feel our best and a good quality dark chocolate can help revive a sense of wellbeing in us all. When choosing dark chocolate, aim for 70 percent Cacao or more. Dark chocolate still contains added sugars and fats, so a small serving of 1 to 3 gram square pieces is appropriate and make sure there is no high-fructose syrup or hydrogenated fats in your chocolate. Try Anti Aging Brand chocolate and nutritional supplements.

Chamomile Unwind After Exercise

Chamomile is one of the most studied plants and many people around the world use chamomile tea as an herbal remedy because of its immune boosting antibacterial, anti-inflammatory, antioxidant and relaxant properties. Chamomile helps stimulate weight loss and is loaded with calcium, potassium that helps prevent muscle cramps while exercising. It helps detox the body by getting rid of fluid retention. A cup of hot chamomile tea before bedtime may help you get a better night of sleep, also. A recent study found that chamomile did reduce anxiety symptoms. However, it did not prevent new episodes of anxiety. Chamomile tea is useful in calming anxiety. It is readily available and safe to use in high doses.

Hemp Tea

Contains CBD which is great for aches and pain relief after exercise and also in helping to ease stress and other ailments. Try Anti Aging Brand chocolate and nutritional supplements.

The Effects of Stress Eating

Stress burns up our vitamin B reserves and then we can suffer from adrenal burn out as a side effect. The body can not distinguish between psychological and physiological stress, it treats both types of stress the same way. Too much stress puts the body into fight-or-flight mode, pulling blood flow away from the organ systems and when we are in that mode our metabolism slows down and since we are not digesting, we could be gaining unwanted weight. Sometimes during times of stress. Luckily, there are plenty of foods rich in B vitamins. Good sources include wholegrain cereals, meat, poultry, eggs, nuts, fish, milk, legumes and fresh vegetables.

Emotional Eating

When people feel anxious and bored and get caught up in stressful emotions, it can trigger a metabolic imbalance and they may be more likely to become vulnerable to emotional eating for comfort. Find healthier activities and things to keep your mind and body busy rather than munching. Avoid emotional eating and binging on comfort foods or alcohol which are high in calories and for the most part unhealthy.

Exercise, Adequate Rest And Beauty Sleep

Exercise decreases insomnia recent research indicates that exercise decreases sleep complaints and insomnia in patients. Proper sleep can help you avoid excess weight gain and, over time, lose weight. A lack of sleep increases your cortisol levels, the stress hormone. Cortisol puts your skin in a pro-inflammatory state. This can mean sullen looking skin and puffiness around the eyes. Ensure that you get eight hours of sleep per night, to lower your cortisol levels and prevent accelerated aging.

Beauty Rest

Inadequate sleep is associated with reduced skin health and proven to accelerate skin aging. Sleep deprived women show signs of premature skin aging. Sleep is a very important part of your anti-aging exercise routine as your body only goes through cell renewal and regeneration in the deepest state of sleep. There are many sleep exercises that can help you relax your mind, other than counting sheep.

How Much Sleep For Exercise Recovery

For exercise recovery it is necessary that you get the recommended 7–9 hours each night, it is important to go to bed at the right time, which may involve rearranging a routine. It's important to:

- be comfortable
- be quite
- be dark
- be relaxed

Your bedroom is the most important room in the house, it's important that it is a quiet space away from noises and that it be free from artificial lights and dark so your brain produces melatonin, the sleep hormone. Its important to have a comfortable bed and to be warm in winter and cool in summer. Your bedroom is a healing environment of the home a place to:

The 5 R's

1. rest,
2. regenerate,
3. recover,
4. repair and
5. relax.

CHAPTER 18
Pre & Post-Workout Recovery Foods

Protein Muscle Power

Protein provides branched chain amino acids for sustained endurance. The "Critical Cluster" branched chain amino acids are used as a powerful source of energy during exercise. The "Critical Cluster" branched chain amino acids are Valine, Arginine, Leucine, Isoleucine, and Glutamine. Protein helps stimulate the release of the anabolic hormones that will promote new muscle formation during exercise and result in an increase in lean body mass and a decrease in fat mass. Arginine plays a major role in stimulating the release of anabolic hormones that promote healthy muscle definition and formation. Arginine can be made by the body from ornithine and is done in maintaining good health and homeostasis. Arginine speeds wound healing and has immunity enhancing benefits. Arginine helps the body best when in a stressed state. Arginine may be used for better muscle formation, reduction of physical stress, and in for developing a strong and healthy immune system. Numerous studies in Olympic athletes have shown the positive effects of supplemental Arginine. Protein helps increase your ability to utilize oxygen, thus helping you sustain high-intensity exercise for a longer period. If you weight training more protein is required to have a protein shake and for up to date information on nutrition visit the American Dietetics Association website.

Green Tea

For a pre-exercise drink try some green tea, it contains an amino acid called theanine, which is a precursor to feel good hormones such as serotonin and dopamine L- theanine elevates levels of GABA, as well as increases serotonin and dopamine levels. It helps with motivation and additionally, L- theanine helps to lower levels of corticosterone stress hormone. As with many natural foods and plants that have incredible health benefits, Green tea is receiving increased scrutiny by those who try to discredit it because they can't profit from its use. The fact is, green tea compounds have a real science-backed effect on mood disorders. Theanine has anti-anxiety and calming effects on the brain chemistry and additionally it offers a natural mild boost of caffeine which can give you a quick energy pick-up, also. Green tea is easy to add to your daily diet. It is a healthier replacement for soft drinks and alcoholic beverages. A human research trial, found that 200 mg of theanine improved self-reported relaxation, increased calmness and reduced tension.

Natural Sources of Theanine:

- Coffee
- Tea
- Guarana
- Yerba Mate
- Mushrooms

Anti-Inflammatory Foods for Better Recovery

Foods containing omega-3 fats are one of the best things that you can eat after your workout to initiate a healthy recovery and reduced inflammation.

- Omega 3 fats
- Black beans
- Berries
- Whole grains
- Spices
- Leafy greens
- Onions
- Dandelion Herb Tea
- Milk Thistle Herb Tea
- Hemp Tea
- Echinacea Tea

It Is Easier To Stay Physically Fit Than To Get Out Of Shape And Have To Diet And Work Hard To Get Fit, Again.

- **Turmeric**

Turmeric is a spice commonly used in Indian and South-East Asian foods. The active ingredient in turmeric is called curcumin. Curcumin is as close to a medicine as any food substance as research shows it is anti-inflammatory, anti-bacterial, anti-viral, anti-tumor, and a whole lot of other positive health benefits. Studies show it helps lower anxiety by reducing inflammation and oxidative stress that often increase in people experiencing mood disorders, such as anxiety and depression. Another study found that an increase of curcumin in the diet also increased DHA and reduced anxiety. Turmeric is easy to add to meals. It has minimal flavor, so goes well in smoothies, curries, and casserole dishes. You can also add it to hot milk or nut milk and honey for a delicious drink.

Easy Tumeric Food Sources:

- Chai Tea
- Curry Dishes

Recommended Daily Allowance (RDA)

For more information about daily dietary requirements visit the american dietary association website.

Special Nutritional Advice

A good diet is imperative to good health. Balance is the key, eat a balanced diet and read my other book, "The Balanced Diet and Lifestyle" and try Anti Aging Brand nutritional supplements.

Calming Cravings & A Voracious Appetite After Exercise

When we exercise it stimulates our appetite. If we are not getting enough minerals and amino-acids for muscle fuel we will experience excessive hunger. Sometimes even if we are not hungry we have cravings and that can be a simple fix, it is likely that you are not getting enough minerals if you crave salt or crunch snacks. We have 5 types of taste-bud senses that need daily satisfaction, sweet, salty, sour, bitter and spicy hot. If you crave spicy food you likely need more zinc. If spicy foods seem too hot you likely have enough zinc. Zinc and magnesium are synergistic and if you get too much of one you can't absorb the other. Zinc is the energy conductor in the body. The body uses zinc to process nutrients.

Make sure you get all the flavors daily and your appetite and your taste buds will be more satisfied with your diet. Go for lower calorie foods with high water content that are more filling, broths, salads and whole fruits such as grapefruit. Avoid processed foods empty of nutrition and filled with preservatives, excess salt, sugar and fat. Also, greatly limit foods such as cheese, pasta and bread. However, a very small half-portion is better than feeling deprived.

Vitamin D & Recovery After Exercise

Vitamin D is the sunshine vitamin, it can help improve lack of motivation for exercise and on the flip it can help muscle recovery after exercise. It's important for strong teeth and bones, also it's good for skin and researchers are increasingly linking vitamin D deficiency to mood disorders, such as depression and anxiety. Research proves that vitamin D positively helps improve signs of depression. Other studies on pregnant women and older adults have also highlighted how vitamin D helps improve mood. Vitamin D may also improve seasonal affective disorder (SAD) during winter and during prolonged indoor states but whenever you can get out and get some fresh air and sunshine, do it. Get outside and soak up vitamin D because the sun naturally stimulates production in your body and it can help keep your body strong to exercise for life.

Fermented Foods & Good Bacteria

Yogurt can be either vegan or dairy based. Dairy has tryptophan and vitamin D but offers many other nutrients, too. Yogurt is a good option for everyone as it can be made from fermented rice, soy, coconut kefir or from and fermented milk products, regardless yogurt contains good bacteria, such as *Lactobacillus* and *Bifidobacteria*. There is emerging evidence that these bacteria and fermented products have positive and calming effects on brain health. Yogurt and other dairy products have an anti-inflammatory effect in the body. Some research suggests that chronic inflammation may be partially responsible for anxiety, stress, and depression and therefore fermented foods are a good exercise support food, too.

Studies have found fermented foods help reduce social anxiety, while multiple studies have found that consuming healthful bacteria increases happiness in people. Add yogurt, coconut aminos and other fermented foods to your diet and try some sauerkraut, pickled onions, fermented soy or tofu and kimchi. All can help benefit your natural gut flora which tend to become depleted with age and a poor diet and it may even help reduce your anxiety and stress, too.

Post Exercise Recovery

Athletic people need extra nutrition. It is important to eat a balanced diet. If you are having problems with meal planning, seek individualized nutritional advice from a professionally trained nutritionist. Additionally, water and hydration is important when we exercise, as exercise makes us perspire and can become dehydrated. Replenish electrolytes after exercise we often sweat. The more you sweat the more nutrients you lose and the greater your risk of developing a nutritional deficiency. The more you work your muscles the more nutrition your body needs to prevent the body from pulling nutrients from the organ systems and nutrient reserves. Everyone needs a proper balance of essential nutrients and should follow a balanced diet according to their daily recommended nutritional requirements. We use our muscles when we exercise. Just two pounds of muscle can burn ten pounds of fat in a year. Therefore, we need muscle fuel for the extra work our muscles do during exercise. Muscle is protein just as meat and flesh is protein.

One of the best foods for an athlete is protein. Protein should be increased in body-building and training diets and proteins are excellent for energy. The enzymes protease and peptidase are needed to properly digest protein. Caution should be used to increase the protein intake to balance your sources of proteins without adding animal sources. Therefore, vegetable proteins such as soy, beans, nuts, whole grains and fish are the best choices. Red Meat proteins such as beef produce acid ash residues which in excess, contribute to unhealthy acid imbalances in the body, and therefore, should be eaten only in moderation. Chicken, Turkey and Fish are better meat choices but still produce acid residues.

Anti-Aging Exercise Recovery Nutrition

Type 1 & II Collagen protein is important for anti-aging benefits. Extra proteins are necessary for athletes and muscle building benefits; however, a person can eat too much protein, a high meat, high acid diet may result in high urea and heavy uric acid concentrations have been linked to deaths in active athletes. Athletes need minerals and amino acids. Mineral deficiencies can lead to strokes in athletes. We sweat out a lot of trace nutrients during intense exercise. That is why I believe it's not healthy to over do exercise, either. Moderation is key. Replenishing essential nutrients is important for the body to maintain good health and proper function. Too much protein is unhealthy and can lead to a buildup of excess urea & acid residues that cause heart stress if the protein is not digested properly. The top exercise recovery supplements are:

- **Multi Amino Acid Protein Supplement** - BCAAs Branched-Chain Amino Acids are pure muscle fuel and the building blocks of protein.

- **Calcium, Magnesium, Potassium-** helps stop and prevent muscle spasms, cramps and soreness and helps to flush out lactic acid.
- **Astaxanthin-** Antioxidants and exercise recovery.
- **Vitamin C-** is needed to make a protein called collagen and is needed for repairing tendons, ligaments and healing surgical wounds.
- **Daily Multi-**Vitamin and Mineral Combo Formula that contains all the essential nutrients with iron and extra B vitamins for energy and stamina.
- **L-Arginine-** is a precursor for nitric oxide that is known to improve blood flow, which in turn may aid stamina and the delivery of important nutrients to **working** muscles and assist with recovery and metabolic waste removal.
- **Water-** is the most important and overlooked, nutrient for athletes.

Your body also needs enzymes from raw plants to digest protein. Anti-Aging Brand protein powder has it all in a balanced formula. Keep in mind, many athletes overdose on protein. Too much of a good thing, is a bad thing. Urea's are the undigested proteins within the body. A sign of high urea in the body are unusual or pronounced deep wrinkles in the forehead area another symptom is feeling fatigued when you wake up in the morning. With all the high protein training food supplements on the market one must be aware of these warning signs to reduce risk of toxic urea levels. If you suspect you may have this problem, consult with your doctor. High protein shakes and food supplements should be used with caution to keep a healthy balance of nutrition by including other healthy foods in your diet. Periodically, one should give the body a rest from the hard digestion of high protein food supplements and allow the body adequate intervals of alkalizing foods and short fast to stimulate autophagy and to offset any imbalance that may be occurring within the body.

Inflammation Causes

- **Injuries-** like scrapes or damage through foreign objects for example a thorn in your finger or a tear in muscle from overworking or over exercising, sports injury.
- **Chemicals** or radiation, in food or the environment.
- **Pathogens-** bacteria, germs, viruses or fungi.

Probiotics, Elimination And Inflammation

Nutrient absorption declines with age, often because of an imbalance of good bacteria and organisms that are needed for optimal digestion. Inflammation can result as a result of a lack of prebiotics and probiotics and cause sluggish metabolism. Probiotics help break down waste for better elimination. Prebiotics help with nutrient utilization and assimilation. There are three trending essential Probiotics proven to restore intestinal health and weight balance.

- **L. gasseri** – A Fat Buster
- **B. breve** – A Metabolism Booster
- **B. lactis** – Flushes Inflammation

C H A P T E R 1 9

Exercise Induced Atophagy

Autophagy Fasting Exercise

Autophagy is the body's internal self-cleaning system. The meaning of the word Autophagy means "Auto" self and "phagy" means eat. Autophagy is the word for "self-eating or a better way to look at it is to fast or do exercises or treatments to trigger and activate our body's own internal self cleaning. During fasting, the process of autophagy initiates after 18-20 hours of fasting, with the maximal benefits occurring after depriving yourself of solid food 48–72 hours, which sounds like misery, but autophagy can be triggered by staying a little bit cold and hungry, too, or by doing short burst high intensity exercise or by consuming miniscule portions of certain food substances such as copious amounts of bergamot tea or lemon water on an otherwise empty stomach.

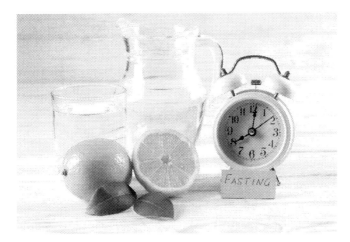

Exercise Induced Autophagy

Recent studies suggest that exercise stimulates autophagy in both muscles and other bodily tissues. Autophagy is our body's own internal self-cleaning mechanism. It's the process that the body eats up all the dead cells to make way for new ones to regenerate and it's important because nobody needs a bunch of dead waste sticking around. Additionally, muscle-derived myokines after exercise help induce autophagy in liver cells.

- The best exercise to stimulate autophagy is by doing a mix of:
  - Resistance training and
  - Short-burst high-intensity interval training
  - Cardio

- Too much exercise negates some autophagy benefits.
  - Only do high intensity exercise only about 30 minutes per day.
  - High intensity exercise is a stressor of the body and mind.
  - It's unnatural to deliberately push yourself into a physical state beyond your capacity and it can cause harm
  - The hippocratic oath to good health care is "first of all do no harm".
  - Exercising yourself beyond your means is an equivalent to being in combat and that is too stressful and damaging to the body.
  - healthy exercise should be uncomfortable but it should never be painful and
  - exercise doesn't have as much anti-aging benefit by pushing your pain threshold or by prolonging a high-intensity state of stress on the body is counter productive and accelerates aging of the joints and musculoskeletal system.

Autophagy Alternatives

Autophagy is automatically stimulated during a fast. However, many people can't fast due to various reasons, low blood sugar or self-control issues. In those cases, there is an alternative approach. Our body goes into autophagy automatically when we feel a little bit hungry or a little bit cold. So in that sense it's always good to feel a little bit cold and hungry.

- Do intermittent fasting for 18 hours overnight through till midday. 7 pm till 12 noon or 8pm-1pm.
- Apply an ice pack to the upper back/in neck area.

Anti-Aging Autophagy

Autophagy is important for Anti-Aging. Our society is all about satiation but staying satiated is overindulgent and can block our autophagy. Some foods that stimulate autophagy are:

- Cinnamon
- Ginseng
- Garlic
- Chaga
- Reishi Mushrooms
- Pomegranate
- Elderberries
- Bergamot Tea
- Berberine
- Resveratrol
- MCT oil
- Coffee
- Green tea
- Turmeric
- Ginger
- Earl Grey Tea

Cooking

Anytime we want to change the molecular structure of something in a laboratory, we heat it up. The same thing happens when we heat foods. When you cook veggies, the heat kills enzymes. Enzymes are important for every function in your body. Never microwave it alters your food's chemistry in a negative way that can cause harm. Microwaving creates known carcinogens called acrylamides in food and beverages. Avoid burning food when cooking, as burning processed meats that are loaded with preservatives, also causes carcinogens to form in your food. Sure have some cooked foods, but let raw, organic non-gmo foods dominate your diet.

Exercise Triggers Glucagon Induced Atophagy

Always keep in mind that in the first 20 minutes of moderate to intense exercise performance, muscle glycogen is used as the primary energy source and provides glucose for muscle fueling. By exercising until your oxygen reserves it will cause your body to use protein out of the muscle to cause a new formation of glucose this is called gluconeogenesis. It is important to exercise longer than 20 minutes to get into the most efficient fat burning phase of exercise. After this initial 20-minute phase of exercise, fatty acids and the branched chain amino acids are the muscle's major energy source. Drink water after exercise and do not eat sugary substances immediately after exercise until the hormones decline or you will crash after your workout because the liver will secrete these hormones.

When you exercise, the body produces hormones that block insulin so your body can effectively use the glucose from your muscles and from the bloodstream. One of the best foods for athletes is protein. Protein should be increased in diets of training athletes. Protein is excellent for increasing energy levels in athletes. The enzymes protease and peptidase are needed to properly digest protein. Caution should be used to increase the protein intake without adding animal sources. Therefore, vegetable proteins such as soy, beans, nuts, whole grains and fish are the best choices. Proteins such as beef & chicken produce acid ash residues which in excess, contribute to unhealthy acid imbalances in the body, and therefore, should be eaten only in moderation. Extra proteins are necessary for athletes however, high urea and heavy uric acid concentrations have been linked to deaths in active athletes. Urea's are the undigested proteins within the body. A sign of high urea in the body are unusual or pronounced deep wrinkles in the forehead area another symptom is feeling fatigued when you wake up in the morning. With all the high protein training food supplements on the market one must be aware of these warning signs to reduce risk of toxic urea levels. Periodically, one should give the body a rest from the hard digestion of these high protein food supplements and allow the body adequate intervals of alkalizing to offset any imbalance that may be occurring within the body.

Example Autophagy Menu & Regimen:

Autophagy is triggered by hunger so after a night's sleep is a good time to periodically allow your body to go into a state of autophagy and allow the body to do its internal self-cleaning. An easy way is to skip breakfast and have a late lunch, drinking only fluids that stimulate autophagy and then breaking the fast with a fresh veggie juice, whole raw fruit, protein shake or a salad. Drink a glass of water 30 minutes before or 30 minutes after eating. You may add lemon cucumber, mint or grapefruit slices to your water.

Morning

Drink 1 glass of water
Drink 1 Cup of black coffee
Drink 3 Cups of Green Tea, Bergamot
Drink 1 Cup of Pea Flower Tea

Late Lunch (after noon)

Collagen Protein Shake or
Small salad

- 1 cup of arugula leaves
- ½ lemon squeezed over leaves
- 1 Tablespoon cranberries or grapes as topper
- 1 Tablespoon of raw seeds or nuts as salad topper
- 1 Tablespoon of Parmesan cheese
- 1 glass of water

Afternoon Snack

- ½ Avocado (large or whole small) or
- ½ Grapefruit or
- ½ cup of yogurt (dairy or non dairy)
- 1oz. dark chocolate (try Anti-Aging Brand)
- 1 glass of water

Dinner

- Steamed Broccoli (or raw)
- 1 Cup Quinoa or Brown rice with
- 1 T. coconut aminos (poured over the rice)
- 3 oz of lean meat or meat alternative
- 1 glass of water

Snack

- 1 apple
- 10 almonds
- 6 olives
- 1 glass of water

Bed Time

- Cup of camomile tea

CHAPTER 20

Do The Work Reap The Reward

You may be thinking, why is there a chapter on this topic? well because it's a fact, you have to do the work to reap the reward. Self-discipline is the most important personal skill that you will ever develop and it will bring everything you do in life closer to success. Self discipline helps you work, it is having the ability to control your actions and overcome your weaknesses. It is the ability to make decisions in your best interest and pursue what is best for you, despite many temptations to abandon it. Adopting discipline to stick to a daily exercise habit is one of the first forms of self-discipline that soldiers are taught in the military. There are many boot-camp and coaching programs that you can join or download online that will greatly improve your workout self-discipline and the more you workout the greater you will develop self-discipline which is one of the main reasons the military sends new cadets to boot-camp.

Release Your Inner Most Physically Fit Self

Why Exercise Is Called A "Work-Out"

Exercise is often referred to as a "work-out" because exercise is a form of work. Working-out is in essence working your body to the point of muscle fatigue or to a physical feeling of using up physical energy. Your body is built to be worked but not beyond the point of exhaustion. When you don't work your body, your body stops working as efficiently. When you don't exercise you become run down, tired, sluggish and sedentary. when you work out you build muscle and 10 pounds of muscle burns 10 pounds of fat within a year. A sedentary lifestyle is the #1 cause of illness and death in the U.S. any way you look at it. Exercise is a life-saver, if you want to look at it that way. Exercise is the most rewarding form of work you can do to maintain your youthful vitality. The more you work-out the more self-discipline you develop. Examples of reward work are:

- **The Work:**
  Wash the dishes and clean up the kitchen before bed, every night.

- **The Reward:**
  You wake up and start your day in a clean organized environment every day, free from dirty dishes and a pile of filth and clutter.

- **The Work:**
  You do your daily exercise plan

- **The Reward:**
  You have an amazing looking body, you look younger than you actually are, you feel stronger and energised and you live a longer, healthier and more active life.

- **The Work:**
  You make your bed up as soon as you arise.

- **The Reward:**
  You have a freshly made bed each night when you lay down to get your regenerative beauty rest.

- **The Work:**
  You exercise and watch your diet.

- **The Reward:**
  You lose weight and look great!

"If you work your muscles enough, you won't have any excess fat on your body"

Fat And Muscle Facts:

Each extra pound of stored fat, makes your heart have to pump through an additional mile of blood vessels. Just 1 pound of muscle will burn 10 pounds of body fat in a year! Therefore, think of the reward you get by losing excess fat and think of how much better your fat metabolism will be if you build 10 pounds of muscle.

- if you work out and build 10 pounds of muscle, that 10 pounds of muscle will burn off 100 pounds of fat in one year! That is a reward!

CHAPTER 21
Kindness, Love & Gratitude Exercises

When we express love, kindness or gratitude or when we receive love, kindness or gratitude our brain releases dopamine and serotonin, the two crucial neurotransmitters responsible for our emotions and these two neurotransmitters give us that instant feel 'good' feeling and the feelings of joy and happiness are often associated with the experience of interacting with feelings of love and kindness.

Whether expressing gratitude for what's good in life or showing gratitude to someone who has helped us in some way, perhaps at work, for example, that is when neural circuitry in our brain (stem) releases dopamine.

Dopamine makes us feel good and triggers positive emotions, we feel optimistic, and it fosters camaraderie. Dopamine and Serotonin elevate our mood immediately, making us feel happier. Research shows gratitude is a strong way to reduce anxiety. Additionally, gratitude has the ability to strengthen relationships, improve mental health, and minimize stress. In fact, researchers suggest that gratitude's effects may be long-lasting and especially positive.

Practice Love Exercises

The hormones your body produces when you are in love are the most healing hormones we produce, oxytocin, serotonin, dopamine and many more energising feel good hormones that give us all strength and vitality.

The world can always use a little more love and kindness, too. Spread the love. Make this year a year of global goodness. When we help others we ultimately help ourselves. Make this a year of love and kindness and global goodness.

Live, Love, Laugh, Life Is Action!

Kindness Exercise

It is a good exercise for the heart to do random acts of kindness. Kindness is doing something lovingly for another. Doing good deeds is an exercise in effort. Make an effort to be kind. To be kind you must first have a feeling of love in your heart as you take action. There are exercises you can do to feel more love and to be more kind. Some will blame their environment for being insensitive to kindness in their community. It is in fact, the level of love within your own heart that allows you to be the kind person you choose to be. We must first be the change we want to see in our communities for change to come. Here are some love and kindness exercises:

- Spread kindness
- Tell the people you love, that you love them
- Show affection to those you love
- Rub someone's upper arms or shoulders if you can't hug them or hold their hands.
- Put down your phone and technology and communicate with members of your household with quality attention.

- Talk kindly to your family members with good eye contact.
- Call your parents and listen to them.
- Call your children to acknowledge what they have to say, sometimes they can enlighten you on their generation's view of the world, today.
- Wave and smile at your neighbor
- Speak kindly to a service attendant
- Help an elderly person across the street
- Help an elderly neighbor roll their trash bin to and from the road.
- Ask people if there is anything you can do for them.
- Be helpful with chores
- Help clean up.
- Give to the homeless
- Support a charity
- Pay for a single working moms kid's dinner
- Pay for orphaned child's school clothes
- Help family members who are struggling when you can.
- If you notice a relative has a dirty car and their working hard offer to wash their car for them.
- Encourage college students who are holding down a job.
- Tell someone they inspire you, if they do.
- Do something to help others with a smile on your face
- Doing good deeds is a form of exercise, too.

It Doesn't Cost You Anything To Be Kind, But Not Being Kind Can Cost You Everything

Gratitude Exercise

Research reveals gratitude can have these seven benefits:

- Gratitude opens the door to more relationships.
- Gratitude improves physical health.
- Gratitude improves psychological health.
- Gratitude enhances empathy and reduces aggression.
- Grateful people sleep better.
- Gratitude improves self-esteem.

Each day, think of 3 things you are grateful for, examples are:

i.   Calming Time In Nature
ii. Favorite People
iii. Good Health

Other Gratitude Exercises

- Start a gratitude calendar.
- Making a commitment to write down good things, daily.
- Notice good things as they happen.
- Practice gratitude rituals.
- Say grace before a meal.

Gratitude exercises and activities are some of the most well-known and proven ways to practice and enhance your gratitude.

- Journaling-
  a. Writing down a few things you are grateful for is one of the easiest and most popular gratitude exercises available.

- Gratitude Jar.
  a. write things you are grateful for on a piece of paper and collect them in a jar.

- Gratitude Rock.
  a. write on a rock things you are grateful for and keep on your nightstand or start a rock garden

- Gratitude Tree.
  a. write things you are grateful for on the leaves.
  b. hang ornaments on the tree and write what you feel grateful for on the ornaments.

CHAPTER 22

Fitness Lifestyle & Your Environment

Your environment is important as it has a direct effect on the lifestyle you live and on your quality of health and longevity. In a national study of nondisabled US adults, inadequate levels of physical activity were associated with an increased risk of premature death. Overall, 8.3% of deaths in nondisabled adults 25 or older were attributed to inadequate levels of physical activity. Smoking and high blood pressure are responsible for the largest number of deaths in the US. Others are dietary, lifestyle, and metabolic risk factors for chronic diseases which also cause a substantial number of deaths in the US.

An unhealthy, sedentary lifestyle is the #1 cause of illness in the U.S.

Death By Sedentary Lifestyle

Sedentary lifestyles increase all causes of mortality, double the risk of cardiovascular diseases, diabetes, and obesity, and increase the risks of colon cancer, high blood pressure, osteoporosis, lipid disorders, depression and anxiety. Yet, you never read the words "Death By Sedentary Lifestyle" on anybody's autopsy report or tombstone.

Effects Of Environment And Relationships

You are only as healthy as your environment. You are usually only as healthy as the 5 people closest to you. Be careful of the friends you chose and the partner you choose to form a family with. If you are single, you will insure yourself to have better health by choosing your intimate partner, wisely. Additionally, your offspring will be affected by Status Quo Behavior (SQB), also. According to public health research, a high SQB was associated with unfavorable health behavior and higher BMI. Targeting SQB might be a promising strategy for promoting healthy behaviors and having a life of better health. Choosing a healthy community to live in is just as important for your family, too. If you have the choice, choose an active lifestyle community to live in.

Exercise Solutions For Unhealthy Lifestyle Behaviors

Exercise is a solution to most unhealthy lifestyle factors.

10 Healthy Lifestyle Factors Are:

- Exercising daily
- Maintaining a healthy weight
- Eating a healthy balanced diet
- Drinking lots of water
- Good Air Quality
- Plenty of sleep
- Avoiding Toxic Exposures
- Not smoking
- Not drinking alcohol
- Keep a regular check on mental and physical health
- Read "The Balance Diet And Lifestyle" by Dr. Joyce Peters to discover a simplified and effective healthy lifestyle plan for anti-aging.

An unhealthy, sedentary lifestyle is the #1 cause of illness in the U.S.

Societal Issues:

Natural Disasters, Pandemics or Social Distancing

Sometimes it is important to have a mental preparedness exercise in place, sort of like a fire drill, for times during natural disasters or if it is required to practice social distancing during a pandemic such as the case of COVID-19.

Coping Solution If Disaster Disrupts Your Lifestyle

Mental preparedness exercises can also help to save lives and in the case of a pandemic can prepare you mentally to take appropriate actions and to help you respond accordingly. In the case of pandemics, staying at home to help in stopping the spread of a contagion, can cause a serious lifestyle disruption that may affect your physical and mental health in a potentially negative way if you are not prepared. Coping skills can help with all crises therefore coping exercises are important to develop coping skills.

Community Teamwork

During times like these, some of the problems of each community must be managed peacefully in a neighborly manner and on an individual level, as well to be a part of the solution, not part of the problem. The problems that our neighbors may face cannot be completely eliminated by a government program alone, everyone must do their part and help those you know in their times of need.

Effects Of Stressful Societal Issues

Developing and using good coping skills is important to get through most every crisis in life. Every community has people dealing with ongoing challenges and when a crisis strikes, for some people, it can worsen alcohol and drug abuse, depression, anxiety, despair and addiction. Additionally, unemployment, poverty, domestic violence and other criminal behavior may increase with a rise in civil unrest. Many of these social risk factors may be improved by reducing social isolation. Joining an online meet-up and staying socially active, online is a good idea. The National Institutes of Health research indicates that the cost of social distancing as a causative factor increases excessive consumption which cost upwards of $500 billion, annually. The Drug enforcement Administration estimated the illicit use of opioid drugs for non-medical purposes is over $53 billion, annually.

Lifestyle Solutions

Studies show people are less likely to turn to substance abuse when they live a healthy lifestyle and are in supportive loving relationships with others and with that being said, social isolation is to be avoided as much as possible.

- Stay in, stay safe but stay physically active and socially inneractive with your friends and family through technology be it online or over the phone.

- There are a plethora of online classes that keep you active, sign up, join in and stay connected to others, it's good for your health.
- Positive psychology is a helpful mind–body practice. Learn and practice the principles of positive psychology on a daily basis, too.
- Do gratitude exercises and share those things you are grateful for with others.
- Prayer and meditation is important, make it a daily practice.
- Talk therapy is important. Talk to your family, friends, loved ones and neighbors and ask how they are feeling and give them you time and attention to share.
- Keep yourself in a positive state of mind.
- Practice Mind–Body exercises daily and share them with others.
- Humanitarian exercises toward your fellow man and the world around you is important all the time, especially during crises.
- Exercise is the body in active motion.
- Life is lived in live action.
- Read the book, the "Balance Diet And Lifestyle" by Dr. Joyce Peters.

CHAPTER 23
Exercise Conclusion

While various exercises offer many benefits and can help you have better health and a better sense of well being throughout your life there are some conditions that will require additional help. If you feel overwhelmed by life's circumstances talk to your doctor, a mental health counselor or other health care provider.

"Life is movement. Life is an exercise"

Exercise can improve many health problems but still, it is not a replacement to regular medical care. Exercise is for everyone and you don't have to pay for a fancy country club or gym membership because many local health departments and social service centers may offer a wealth of information and free healthy lifestyle fitness programs to the public for free in your area. Everyone has good days and days when they feel off. You're not alone but having an effective way to work through it and help bring yourself back to balance, is important and exercise can often serve as the magic key to better health. Life is not about being sedentary, death is. When we don't get all the cells moving, our body becomes sluggish, slows down and eventually dies.

Exercise helps keep us moving and alive. Additionally, throughout life, it takes a village of healthcare providers working together with you as good health occurs through a healthy lifestyle and effort to maintain good health by keeping consumption of unhealthy things to a minimum and healthy foods and substances in moderation, making healthy choices in all you do. Having exercise partners can help keep you motivated to stick to a healthy lifestyle which includes daily exercise. With a healthy balanced lifestyle and daily exercises, you can stay safe, strong and well throughout life.

The Closest Thing To A Magic Anti-Aging Pill, is Exercise!

What The Bible Says About Exercise

God wants you to be healthy because your body is the temple of God and the holy spirit dwells within us. Therefore, Honor God with your body. 1 Corinthians 6:12. Other than bodily exercises the most important exercise in the bible is the daily practice of exercising your faith. To exercise your faith and build spiritual muscles to perfect your faith. Heb 12: 2

CONGRATULATIONS!
May God Bless You To Stay Safe & Stay Well.

If your goal is to lose weight, fast, this CD is the quickest and easiest way! The Anti-Aging Mind-Body Weight Loss CD works fast utilizing self-hypnosis for an energized and slimmer new you. Behavior modification helps you keep the weight off by helping you give up bad eating habits and helps curb cravings for sugar and junk foods. Home hypnosis behavior reprogramming really works! Self-Hypnosis is deemed the most effective method for lasting behavior modification. The Anti-Aging Mind Body Weight Loss Program helps you stay motivated to exercise for life.

A Mind–Body Exercise Plan by Joyce Peters, PhD

Fitness Model Credits:

Summer Perry

Joyce Peters

ABOUT THE AUTHOR

Joyce Peters, PhD

Joyce is the author of many clinical health and wellcare programs, her specialty is in patient adherence and wellcare programs. Joyce's programs have been used in many clinics, hospitals and doctor's offices, throughout the United States and other countries around the world. She provides care for many celebrity clients, also. Additionally, she had a very humble start in the southeast and understands and embraces diversity in America's mixed culture. Dr. Joy has written patient adherence plans for the second largest medical technology platform in the world spanning across 4 continents in 4 languages. She served as a wellness programs consultant and advisor for Mr. Herman Rappaport, an advisor to five U.S. presidents. She was also the director of weight loss programs of a large chain of plastic surgery centers in southern California and before that she was a fitness manager for a chain of women's gyms in southern California. She is affiliated with several prestigious clinics across the nation where her programs are being utilized in a clinical setting on four continents and she personally adapted the original 3 quick and easy exercises to help reduce disaster stress and restore the health and well being of disaster victims for use during the shelter-in-place crisis during COVID-19. This exercise plan is complete, safe and effective and it is the only one you will ever need to stay healthy and fit throughout your lifetime. The only thing you need to do, is this!

"You will have a positive, mind-soothing, health-improving life-changing experience each time you practice these Mind-Body Exercises."

Words From Former President Trump Success

"Most people fail because they quit, because they just don't have "stick-to-itiveness". Love what you do, and do what you love, but, do it with passion! Work at it! Never quit and never give up! The key to success is to develop stick-to-itiveness. Learn to develop stick-to-itiveness and you will be successful in all you do." Donald Trump (quote made to the author, 2005

"...be best, be passionate about all you do" Melania Trump

Exercise Often During Pandemic
Shelter In Place Orders

Stay In, Stay Safe, But, Stay Active

**Complete 30 Minute Mind-Body Workout Routine
3 Steps To Look More Youthful
& Feel Better In 3 Days!**

FINAL WORDS FROM THE AUTHOR

I hope you enjoy this exercise plan and use it to achieve your best self-image. I recommend that you read my other books for more Anti-Aging tips. This exercise plan offers great benefits for both your Mind and Body. I designed the 3 exercises for my patients who are often so busy with life that it was difficult for them to find time for exercise, especially my celebrity clients who are always traveling and in need of exercises they can do consistently while on-the-go, flying around the world. All of my patients love it and hopefully, so will you. This plan was edited during covid-19 and redesigned for the purpose of helping shelter-in-place victims stay fit at home. You can improve your posture and physical fitness anywhere, anyplace and anytime in 15-30 minutes a day and you don't need a gym to do this plan. It's the perfect in-home exercise plan for you and for those who are seeking a quick, easy, safe and effective at home exercise plan. The 3 main exercises are all you need to tighten and tone every major muscle group in your body. These 3 exercises are quick, easy, safe and effective. Going to the gym is great. Having cool workout clothes is nice, too, but the good news is, you don't need anything to do this plan and get in the best shape of your life, now. Develop stick-to-it-tiveness and do these 3 exercises and you will see results within 3 days with even greater improvements over time. President Donald Trump made the above quote to me specifically, when I asked him for advice on developing this program and a chain of fitness centers. His advice to me, were words of wisdom that you can also apply to your exercise success, too, by doing the 30 minute Anti-Aging Exercise plan, daily. In the words of former president Obama, "yes, we can"! You can apply a can-do mindset to your fitness motivation attitude and it will help you get in shape. I hope this complete exercise plan helps you make your total fitness the best it's ever been.

Joyce Peters, PhD,
Fitness Trainer, Exercise Plan Creator, Author.

Joyce Peters PhD, CFT, CNC, CMT, CHT

RESEARCH REFERENCES

American College of Sports Medicine
Sports Science Review
The American Health Research Institute
Aerobics and Fitness Association of America–AFAA
American Sports Research Institute
University of Alabama Birmingham UAB
University of California UCLA
The World Health Organization
The International Health Organization
The Centers for Disease Control and Prevention CDC
The National Centers for Disease Control
The National Institutes of Health
The US Department of Agriculture
The US Department of Health and Human Services
The Health Keepers Alliance
The National Foundation for Alternative Medicine
American Obesity Association
American Heart Association
American Naturopathic Medical Association
American Hypnosis Association
Hypnosis Motivation Institute
American Psychotherapy and Medical Hypnosis Association
American College of Alternative Medicine
National Association for Natural Health Care Practitioners
The Coalition for Natural Health Care Professionals
The U.S. Department of Agriculture/National Agricultural Library-USDA

The U.S. Department of Health and Human Services
The Surgeon General's Report
Weight-Control Information Network (WIN)
National Institute of Diabetes,
Digestive, and Kidney Diseases
The Food and Drug Administration-
Trinity College of Natural Health
The Upledger Institute-
Osteopathic Cranial-Sacral Therapy
The Upledger Institute- Somato-Emotional Release
Parker, Life & Palmer Chiropractic Colleges
The Alabama State Chiropractic Association-
The University of Texas-Addiction Science Research
Parker Chiropractic College- Resource Foundation
American College Of Sports Medicine
AFAA American Aerobics and Fitness Association
California State-Long Beach-
AFAA Fitness Trainer Program
Vanderbilt University- AFAA Personal Fitness Trainer Program
HCFA - Alternatives in Patient Care Compliance Law
Clinical Laboratory International Association
National Institute for Natural Health

This book was adapted as a special addition during the Covid-19 pandemic as a Shelter-In-Place exercise program for government contractor submission for use in military shelter-in-place public health programs.